Murder With Love

A Thriller

Francis Durbridge

SAMUELFRENCH-LONDON.CO.UK
SAMUELFRENCH.COM

FOR AMATEUR PRODUCTION ENQUIRIES

UNITED KINGDOM AND WORLD
EXCLUDING NORTH AMERICA
plays@SamuelFrench-London.co.uk
020 7255 4302/01

Each title is subject to availability from Samuel French,

depending upon country of performance.

MURDER WITH LOVE

First produced by Mark Furness at the Theatre Royal, Windsor, on March 2nd, 1976, with the following cast of characters:

Larry Campbell	David Sterne
Jo Mitchell	Jenny Till
Mrs Bedford	Patricia Moore
Ernest Foster	Peter Myers
David Ryder	Peter Byrne
George Rudd	Michael Howe
Roy Campbell	Mike Hall
Clare Norman	Ann Kennedy
Cleaver	Dermot Walsh

The Play directed by Hugh Goldie
Setting by John Page

The action takes place in the living-room of Larry Campbell's flat and the drawing-room of David Ryder's house, in London

ACT I Monday morning
           Monday evening
           Monday night
           Tuesday morning

ACT II Thursday morning
           Friday morning
           Friday afternoon

Time—the present

ACT I

The stage is divided into two rooms, separated by a broken wall running down C. *Monday morning*

The room R *is the drawing-room of David Ryder's house. It is comfortable, well furnished, and faintly untidy. This is not surprising since it is serving a dual purpose at the moment, that of living-room and chambers. There are several nice chairs, including a red leather wing-chair; plenty of books, and two or three good pictures. A desk, bearing papers, telephones, and several photographs, stands at right angles to the only door, which leads to the hall and the rest of the house. At the back of the room full-length curtains conceal long windows*

The room L *is the living-room of Larry Campbell's flat in Curzon Street. This is the last remaining apartment in a building now devoted to offices. The room has been furnished by an interior decorator with an obvious liking for "things" Swedish. A drinks cabinet stands on the side wall* L *next to a door which leads to the main bedroom and the rest of the flat. There are several curiously shaped lamps and chairs together with a settee and a long low table bearing telephone, magazines, cigarettes, etc. The only window is back* C *forming a bay which is part of an alcove. In the alcove stands a television set and an easy-chair. The front door of the flat is through a tiny hall* L *of the alcove*

Both rooms are in darkness. After a moment the Lights come up on the living-room of Larry Campbell's flat. The hall door opens and Larry enters carrying a suitcase, a valise, and several magazines. His folded overcoat is draped over his shoulders. Larry Campbell is an attractive, self-possessed man and everything about him is symptomatic of his recent stay in the United States. Well-cut trousers supported by crocodile belt; cream shirt with monogram "LC" on the breast pocket; knitted tie; tiny gold tie-clip. He drops his things on to a chair and, crossing to the drinks cabinet, pours himself a drink. Before drinking, he takes a tablet from his pocket and swallows it. Having swallowed the tablet he then opens his suitcase and produces a large bronze statuette in the shape of a naked woman. He puts the figure on the drinks cabinet and moving back several paces, stands quietly admiring it. Pause. He slowly comes to the conclusion that the figure will look better elsewhere and, with a shake of the head, he picks up the statuette and the suitcase and valise, and goes into the bedroom

The telephone rings

After a moment Larry comes out of the bedroom and goes to the telephone

Larry (*on the telephone*) Hello? . . . Yes, Larry Campbell speaking. . . . Who? . . . (*Irritatedly*) My—what? My brother! Put him on. . . . (*After a moment*) Roy, how are you? I've just this minute arrived. . . . No, Clare isn't here, I understand she's rehearsing. . . . I sound what? . . . It's not surprising, the journey was pretty tiring and we were three hours late leaving New York. . . . Roy, when am I going to see you? . . . As soon as possible, I'm flying back to the States at the end of the week. . . . Yes, I have—I've done a very good deal. I'll tell you all about it when I see you. Yes, that's fine. See you then . . .

Larry replaces the receiver and picks up a pad which is by the telephone. He reads through the various messages on the pad then helps himself to a cigarette from the box on the table. He is about to light the cigarette when he suddenly changes his mind and picks up the telephone again. He stands for a moment, hesitating, not sure whether to make the call or not; finally he dials

(*On the telephone*) . . . This is four-nine-nine seven-eight-six-three. . . . I wish to send a telegram. The subscriber's name is Campbell. . . . Yes, that's right, Campbell. . . . (*Pause*) . . . It's to—Miss Jo Mitchell. . . . Jo, J.O. . . . Mitchell. . . . M.I.T.C.H.E.L.L. . . . That's right. *Sunday News*, Fleet Street, E.C. four. . . . (*Slight pause*) . . . "Can think of six thousand reasons why we should meet. Contact me immediately. Larry Campbell." . . . Yes, that's right—thank you . . .

Larry puts down the telephone, crosses to the settee, and lies down. He is rearranging the cushions and making himself comfortable when the room gradually dims out

The Lights slowly rise on David Ryder's room. It is the evening of the same day

Jo Mitchell is sitting in the wing-chair reading a newspaper. Jo is a journalist and is responsible for a widely read gossip column. In spite of a slightly masculine manner and a somewhat severe style of dress she is a sympathetic person and is well liked in Fleet Street

Mrs Bedford, David Ryder's housekeeper, enters

Mrs Bedford Mr Ryder's just come in, Miss Mitchell. He's got a Mr Foster with him, but I don't think he'll be long .

Jo Thank you, Mrs Bedford. How are things progressing at Lincolns Inn?

Mrs Bedford They're not, I'm afraid! I don't know whether Mr Ryder's told you but the builders are now having trouble with the staircase.

Jo rises and, moving to the desk, puts down the newspaper

Jo The staircase? I thought it was the fireplace?

Mrs Bedford No, that was last week. And the week before it was the ceiling. And the week before that it was the floorboards. And the week before—it just never stops!

Jo I'm afraid there's always trouble with those old buildings.

Mrs Bedford The way things are going I doubt very much whether Mr Ryder will be back in his Chambers by this time next year.

Ernest Foster comes into the room. He is a fastidiously dressed lawyer in his middle forties

Ernest (*surprised*) Jo! My dear, how nice to see you! (*To Mrs Bedford*) You never told me Miss Mitchell was here!

Mrs Bedford I didn't know you were acquainted, Mr Foster.

Ernest Miss Mitchell and I are very old friends. I criticize her column every Sunday morning, don't I, Jo?

Jo Every Sunday morning! I do wish you'd go back to playing golf on a Sunday, Ernest.

Ernest I wouldn't dream of it. I find the literary exercise far more stimulating. Besides, it enables me to stay in bed longer.

Mrs Bedford Did Mr Ryder win the case, sir?

Ernest (*nodding*) Yes, he won. It's all over, thank goodness.

Mrs Bedford Mr Ryder will be pleased.

Mrs Bedford smiles at Jo, and goes out

Jo Is that the chorus girl case?

Ernest Yes—the plaintiff was a client of mine. (*Looking at her*) You've lost weight, Jo.

Jo Well, thank heavens it's noticeable! I've been practically living on orange juice. It's a wonder I haven't turned into an orange.

Ernest It suits you. You look better for it. Wish I could persuade my wife to go on a diet. She's far too heavy and she eats like a horse. Usually between meals.

Jo How is your wife? I haven't seen her for ages.

Ernest Oh—she's all right, considering.

Joe (*after a slight hesitation*) And Janet?

Ernest Janet? She's fine. (*After a moment, looking at her*) Did—David tell you?

Jo (*quietly*) No, but I heard about it, from someone else.

Ernest Oh. (*A tiny pause*) It was quite a shock, Jo.

Jo Yes, I'm sure it was.

Ernest My wife was the one I felt sorry for. Damn sorry. She and Janet have always got on well together. Always confided in each other. It's a bit of a cliché, I know, but they really are more like sisters than mother and daughter. (*With a resigned shrug*) Well—there you are. We live in a permissive society.

Jo Janet's determined to have the child?

Ernest Absolutely determined. Mention the word abortion in our house, and all hell's let loose!

Pause

Jo Who's the man, Ernest, do you know?

Ernest She hasn't told us and she's obviously not going to. We've tried to find out, of course. But it's no use, I'm afraid. Her friends just won't talk. (*After a moment*) Is David taking you out to dinner?

Jo Well, he's supposed to be, but we had a date last Saturday and he forgot all about it. He's terribly forgetful these days.

Ernest Yes, I know, but I'm afraid he wasn't at all well last week. He caught a bug of some kind. Looked awful. The poor devil kept feeling sick the whole time.

Jo Oh! I didn't know that.

Ernest That's just between you and me, Jo! You know what he's like. He hates a fuss of any kind. As a matter of fact, I don't think he's a hundred per cent now. He didn't look too good in Court this morning.

Jo He works too hard.

Ernest (*nodding*) I suppose that's inevitable, under the circumstances. (*Taking out his cigarette case*) You should try and talk him into taking a holiday.

Jo Don't you think I've tried? He just won't listen to me.

Ernest offers Jo a cigarette, but she shakes her head. As he lights his cigarette he glances down at a photograph on the desk

Ernest (*indicating the photograph*) I haven't seen this one before.

Jo Yes, you have. It's a new frame, that's all. It used to be in the dining-room.

Ernest (*after a pause, still looking at the photograph*) When was it taken?

Jo Just before she left him.

Ernest picks up the photograph and looks at it

Ernest Well—she was a damn good-looking woman, there's no doubt about that. (*He puts down the photograph*) It's funny, you know, although I've known David for years, I only met his wife once—and that was at the theatre.

Jo You'd have liked her, Ernest. She was awfully good company and terribly kind.

Ernest (*surprised*) Kind?

Jo That surprises you?

Ernest In view of what happened, it certainly does. I was in Scotland when the boy was killed. I remember buying a paper and seeing a picture of David and his wife on the front page. At first I just didn't believe it. Then when I got back to London a cousin of David's told me the whole story. At least, her version of it.

Jo It's surprising how many there've been.

Ernest Yes, I know. Jo, how did she first meet this chap—Larry Campbell?

Jo Well, I suppose indirectly I was responsible. When I started the column the paper threw a party for me. I invited Evelyn and David and someone —I don't know who it was—asked Larry. He was with one of the advertizing agencies at the time.

Ernest Did you think they'd fallen for each other?

Jo No, it never occurred to me. But a week or two later I drove down to Bournemouth to do an interview and I stopped at the Chewton Glen. They were in the cocktail bar.

Ernest But didn't she talk to David? Didn't she tell him . . .?

Jo She didn't tell him anything. She simply sent the child out with the *au-pair* one morning, packed her bag, and—that was it.

Ernest She wasn't very kind on that occasion, was she?

Jo (*quietly*) No, Ernest, she wasn't.

Ernest Where did she die, Jo? There were so many conflicting reports.

Jo She was taken ill in Monte Carlo but they rushed her to a hospital just outside Nice. After the operation she asked to see the boy and the surgeon telephoned David. You know what happened. David flew out with Jonathan and picked up a car at the airport.

Ernest nods

The car hit a lorry and the child was killed. (*After a moment*) Evelyn and I were on the *Sunday Mail* together. She was a secretary in the accounts department. We shared rooms—or rather a room—at the top of an old house in Fitzroy Square. I can remember the first time she met David. She'd been up to Cambridge for the week-end and she came bursting into that room on the Monday morning—and my God was she starry-eyed! She just couldn't stop talking about him! A fortnight later they were married. (*She turns away from him*) If I hadn't invited them to that bloody party she probably would never have heard of Larry Campbell.

Ernest (*indicating the newspaper*) I don't know whether you've seen it or not, but there's a photograph of him in tonight's paper. He's just re-turned from America.

Jo Yes, I've seen it.

Ernest He seems to be running true to form. According to all accounts he's now got himself engaged to a millionaire's daughter.

Jo It's probably just publicity.

Ernest Probably. Curiously enough, I met his brother about a week or so ago.

Jo Roy?

Ernest That's right. He came to see me about making a Will. Odd sort of chap, I thought. As a matter of fact, I didn't realize who he was until after he'd left. It was Janet who told me he was Larry Campbell's brother.

Jo Does Janet know Larry?

Ernest (*thoughtfully*) Well—yes. I suppose she must do.

David Ryder enters. He is a distinguished-looking man with a thoughtful, preoccupied manner. He stares at Jo in astonishment

David Why, Jo, my dear! This is a surprise!

Jo (*to Ernest, laughing*) See what I mean? (*To David*) You're supposed to be taking me out to dinner!

David Yes, of course! (*Kissing Jo*) I hadn't forgotten——

Jo You could have fooled me!

David —I've booked a table at the Hilton.

Jo Oh! Don't let's go to a hotel, David. Couldn't we go to Luigi's?

David (*after a momentary hesitation*) I had lunch at Luigi's . . .

Ernest (*surprised*) You did nothing of the sort!

David (*ignoring Ernest's remark*) I'm told the Hilton's awfully good these days, Jo. You'll like it. (*Changing the subject*) We did very well this afternoon, didn't we, Ernest?

Ernest We certainly did. Incidentally, the old boy was delighted. He says it's resuscitated his belief in the infallibility of British Justice.

David Well, as long as it hasn't resuscitated his belief in the infallibility of the British Call Girl, I don't mind. (*To Jo*) It's always the same when you're dealing with blackmail.

Mrs Bedford appears in the doorway

If he'd had the guts to stand up to her in the first place she'd never have brought the case. (*Turning*) What is it, Mrs Bedford?

Mrs Bedford Excuse me, sir. A Mr Rudd is here. He says he's got an appointment.

David Rudd? Ah, yes! Of course. Ask him to wait a few minutes.

Mrs Bedford goes out

Ernest That wouldn't be George Rudd, by any chance?

David That's right. He wrote me a letter, said he'd like to see me.

Ernest Yes, and I know what it is he wants to see you about! He's got a nerve, that boy. He rang me up about a fortnight ago. Said he was thinking of emigrating and would I be good enough to lend him five hundred pounds.

David And did you?

Ernest (*laughing*) Why do you think he's coming to see you?

David Rudd's all right—he had an unlucky break, that's all.

Ernest Yes, that's what I thought at the time. Now I'm not so sure. (*To Jo*) He used to work for Milton's, the safe people. He broke into a house on Putney Heath.

David He was *accused* of breaking into a house on Putney Heath.

Ernest (*laughing*) Yes, all right, have it your own way! But fancy coming to you, of all people! If you hadn't got him off the hook he wouldn't be in a position to emigrate.

David Well, he isn't now, by the sound of things. (*He looks at his watch*) Jo, I'll be about half an hour. I'd like to change after I've seen this chap.

Ernest (*to Jo*) Come along, I'll buy you a triple orange juice and tell you how to write that column of yours.

Jo Half an hour, David—no longer! Please!

David (*laughing and holding up his hand as if taking the oath*) No longer, Jo—I promise.

Jo goes out, followed by Ernest

David crosses the room and stands by the desk for a moment, deep in thought. Then, glancing down, he notices the newspaper. He picks up the paper and looks at the picture of Larry Campbell

George Rudd enters. Rudd is twenty-eight, but looks younger. His clothes are neat and tidy, but not in very good taste. He watches David for a second or two, and then gives a little cough, in order to attract his attention

(*Suddenly looking up*) Oh—sit down, Rudd.

David goes and sits in the chair facing the desk

Rudd (*sitting in the armchair; with the faint suggestion of a North Country accent*) Was that Mr Foster?

David Yes. Did he speak to you?

Rudd Just said good evening, that's all. I rang him up a couple of weeks ago.

David Yes, I know. He's just been telling me about it. I wish you'd mentioned it before, Rudd.

Rudd Didn't think it was important. (*Smiling*) I tried to borrow five hundred quid from him. The suggestion didn't go down very well, I'm afraid.

David Did you think it would?

Rudd Oh, I dunno. I'm always optimistic. (*Smiling*) Not to worry.

David What did you want the money for?

Rudd (*puzzled by the question*) You know what I wanted it for—to emigrate. Go to Canada.

David (*watching Rudd, quietly*) Oh, yes.

Rudd (*puzzled by David's manner*) Why, we talked about it the other night—in the pub—don't you remember?

David Yes, I remember.

Rudd rises and moves down to the desk

Rudd (*obviously worried*) You haven't changed your mind, have you, Mr Ryder?

David No, I haven't changed my mind, Rudd—but I'm a little perturbed.

Rudd Oh—what about?

David About you. I'm wondering if there's anything else you haven't told me.

Rudd Why no, of course not! Why should there be anything else? I just didn't think it was worth mentioning, that's all. (*A moment's pause; he is still faintly embarrassed*) About Mr Foster, I mean.

David continues to look at Rudd

I'd do anything for you, Mr Ryder. You know that. Good God, if it hadn't been for you I don't know what would have happened to me.

David I think you do, Rudd. (*After a pause*) Did you get the key?

Rudd (*faintly relieved by the change of subject*) Yes. Yes, sure. (*He takes a Yale key out of his pocket and puts it down on the desk*)

David picks it up and looks at it

David Does it work?

Rudd (*laughing, partly to give himself confidence*)   'Course it works. Wouldn't be much use if it didn't, would it?

David You've tried it?

Rudd Yes.

David When?

Rudd Last night. It worked a treat. (*Leaning towards the desk; not unpleasantly*) Look, Mr Ryder, I know this is none of my business—but why do you want the key? Why do you want to get into that flat?

David (*after a moment*) The girl who lives there is suing a friend of mine for divorce. There are certain—photographs I'd like to get hold of.

Rudd Oh, I see.

David (*holding up the key*) Does anyone else know about this?

Rudd No.

David You made it yourself?

Rudd Yes, 'course I did

David You say, you tried the key last night?

Rudd That's right. I watched the flat for a couple of hours. I saw the girl go out so I nipped in and tried it.

David Did anyone see you?

Rudd No.

David You're sure, Rudd?

Rudd Yes, I'm positive. They're mostly offices in that building anyway. The place is dead after six o'clock.

David When did you first go to the flat—to examine the lock?

Rudd A couple of days ago; after we'd had our little talk. (*Shaking his head*) No-one saw me. It was five a.m. (*Grinning*) Not to worry, Mr Ryder.

David nods, hesitates, then puts the key in his pocket, and takes out an envelope

David (*offering Rudd the envelope*) Here's the ticket I promised you. You leave London tomorrow morning. Twelve o'clock. Air Canada. Flight AC eight-five-seven.

Rudd (*rising; a shade nervously*) Tomorrow morning?

David (*surprised by Rudd's reaction*) Yes. You said you had your visa. You told me you were ready to go immediately. I asked you that.

Rudd Yes—yes, sure. That's all right. (*Looking at the envelope*) It's just that, well—I've thought about this so much, talked about it such a lot, I . . . Well, you know how it is . . . (*Taking the envelope, smiling*) Still, not to worry.

David rises and comes round the desk

David Good luck, Rudd.

Rudd Thanks, Mr Ryder. Thanks for everything. (*He hesitates, as if to shake hands, then turns and crosses to the door*)

Rudd exits

David follows him to the door and watches him go out, then he locks the door and returns to the desk. He sits at the desk, unlocks one of the drawers, and produces a cigar box. He opens the box and takes a revolver out of it. He examines the gun, making sure it is loaded, then obviously satisfied he puts it down on the desk and picks up the photograph of his wife. He is looking at this photograph when the Lights begin to dim down on him, finally fading completely

A door bell is heard ringing as the Lights start to come up on Larry Campbell's flat

> *Larry comes out of the bedroom, putting on his jacket as he does so, and crosses into the hall. We hear the front door open*

Roy (*off*) Hello, Larry. Sorry I'm late . . .
Larry (*off*) Roy! How nice to see you! Come along in . . .

> *Larry returns with Roy Campbell. Roy is slightly older than his brother; a tired-looking man wearing a duffle coat and carrying an attaché case*

Roy, it sure is great to see you again! But I was expecting you this afternoon. You said four o'clock.
Roy Yes, I know, but I had to go over to Slough. I've been repairing a television set for a friend of Dilys's.
Larry Well, you're here, that's the main thing! (*He stands back, looking at him*) Let's take a good look at you. (*A moment's pause*) You look tired.
Roy I haven't been very well—we've all had a bug of some kind. Don't you remember, I wrote you about it?
Larry Yes, of course! How is that sister-in-law of mine—is she any better?
Roy Dilys is all right, but the kids have been very poorly. They're on the mend now, thank goodness.
Larry Take your coat off, Roy. I'll get you a drink.

Roy hesitates, then moves into the room and puts down the attaché case

Roy (*rather ill at ease, uncertain of himself*) I haven't a lot of time—so I won't have a drink, if you don't mind.
Larry (*smiling, turning*) You don't have to have one.
Roy Where's Clare?
Larry She's still at the television studio. She's been rehearsing all day. She's recording a show tonight. I think it's nine-fifteen—I'm not sure.
Roy Oh, yes, that's right. It's the Billy West Show. She's done two or three of them. You haven't seen her, then?
Larry No, not yet. She hasn't been able to get away. But I've spoken to her, she telephoned me.
Roy (*hesitantly*) Larry, it's none of my business, but—you're not going to walk out on Clare, are you?
Larry I'm not going to walk out on anyone! Whatever gave you that idea?
Roy There's been quite a bit in the papers just recently about you and that American girl.

Larry Beth Sherman? (*With a laugh, just managing to control his irrita-tion*) You know as well as I do you can't believe everything you read in the newspapers. Nine times out of ten it's just bull.

Roy Well, Clare's worried. Very worried. She's talked to Dilys about it. And Dilys told her to . . .

Larry (*annoyed*) I'm not interested in what Dilys told her! Dilys is your wife, not mine! In any case, she hates my guts. She always has done.

Roy (*reproachfully*) Larry, you know that's not true! Dilys is very fond of you.

Larry (*sorry he made the remark*) Look, we haven't seen each other for ages! Don't let's quarrel, there's a good guy.

Roy (*quietly*) All right.

There is a pause. Larry realizes that his brother is still slightly put out by his remarks

Larry I hate to say this, Roy, but I've worked myself to a standstill during the past three months. I damn nearly had a coronary. And for what? For you and Dilys and the kids. (*Shaking his head*) For nobody else.

Roy Larry, we know you've been working hard!

Larry (*taking the initiative*) Have you ever tried to sell anything in the States?

Roy You know I haven't.

Larry Do you think it was easy trying to peddle that invention of yours?

Roy No, I don't . . .

Larry For twelve solid weeks I hawked that effing contraption from one lousy office to another. And it was always the same story—not interested!

Roy (*puzzled*) But the Americans have been trying to produce a similar machine for years.

Larry You tell them that! You just try and tell them that! After six weeks I was desperate; damn nearly exhausted. I very nearly caught the first plane home. Then one day a friend of mine introduced me to Beth Sherman. I'd already tried to see her old man—Walter Sherman, one of the most influential men in the Middle West—but I couldn't get within a mile of him. (*Grinning*) Anyway, I won't bore you with the lurid details of my association with Miss Sherman—suffice it to say, three days after meeting her I was in the Chicago headquarters of Sherman International, demonstrating your machine to the most hatchet-faced set of bastards you've ever laid eyes on.

Roy (*laughing*) Larry, you're incorrigible! You really are!

Larry (*moving to the table and picking up a large envelope*) And praise the Lord, your brother was on the ball that morning! The adrenalin flowed and the jolly old charisma—what's left of it—worked overtime.

Roy Meaning what, Larry?

Larry (*returning to him*) Meaning, my dear Roy, that in twelve months from now—less than twelve months if we're lucky—that invention of yours will be in production. (*He opens the envelope and hands Roy a document*) Roy, I want you to sign this. It's just a simple, straight-forward agreement. Read it. (*He takes out his pen*)

Roy looks at the document and, watched by Larry, slowly reads it. Pause

Roy (*looking up*) I don't understand. This is an agreement between you and me . . .

Larry (*pleasantly*) That's right.

Roy Why between you and me, Larry?

Larry Roy, for weeks I've been talking—negotiating in fact—without any real authority. I've literally sold something which doesn't belong to me. I trust you of course. I trust you implicitly. But supposing something happens to you? Supposing you get knocked down by a bus?

Roy Yes, but surely, if I sign this agreement . . .

Larry Look, let me explain! At the moment I've got three—two hundred thousand dollars . . .

Roy (*taken aback*) Two hundred thousand dollars!

Larry Yes. Didn't I tell you that?

Roy (*still stunned*) No . . .

Larry I'm sorry! After my Chicago meeting Walter Sherman bought an option from me. He paid two hundred thousand dollars for it. Now that's your money, Roy, every buck, every cent of it! But the cheque was made out to me personally so I had no alternative but to open an account in New York in my name. Now obviously I've got to get that money transferred over here . . .

Roy But that's not difficult, surely?

Larry It's not difficult, but it's not as simple as it sounds. As soon as I get back to the States I've got to contact the American tax people—and you can imagine what they're like! The first thing they'll want from me is proof that you exist and obviously the best proof I can give them is this agreement. Signed and sealed by both of us.

Roy hesitates, then looks at the agreement again. Larry offers him his pen.

Pause

There's still a hell of a lot to do over there, Roy. This is only the beginning.

Another pause. Roy is still staring at the agreement

Roy (*nervously*) Would you have any objection if I showed this to someone?

Larry You mean Dilys?

Roy No, I don't mean Dilys. I met a lawyer about a week ago, a man called Foster. He seemed a very nice chap. Most helpful. I went to see him about making a Will . . .

Larry Roy, if you bring lawyers in on this they'll make a meal of it!

Roy I wasn't suggesting that.

Larry Well—what were you suggesting?

Roy (*looking at the document again; embarrassed*) I just thought it might be a good idea, for both our sakes, if we, well—got someone else to take a look at this, that's all.

Larry (*not unreasonably*) All right, if that's the way you want it. Talk to this guy Foster. Let him have a look at it. But I must warn you, if he takes a long . . . (*He stops dead; he stares at his brother*) Foster, did you say?

Roy Yes.

Larry (*incredulously*) Not Ernest Foster?

Roy I think his name's Ernest, I'm not sure.

Larry "Foster, Kilburn and Jackson"? Southampton Row?

Roy Yes, that's right . . .

Larry Good God Almighty! Who put you on to Ernest Foster? (*Amused*) It'll take him six months to read the contract and even then he won't understand it! Someone's given you a bum steer, Roy. Truthfully. The man's a tortoise!

The telephone rings

Roy (*puzzled; softly*) He didn't strike me like that, Larry.

Larry looks at the telephone, hesitates, then with his eyes still on his brother, and obviously irritated by the interruption, he crosses and picks up the telephone. Roy, somewhat embarrassed by Larry's remarks, stands staring down at the document

Larry (*on the telephone*) Hello? . . . Yes—speaking. . . . Jack—who? (*Surprised*) Jack Keller? . . .

Roy looks up, recognizing the name

I'm fine. . . . No, I'm sorry we can't, I'm all tied up and I'm returning to the States at the end of the week. . . . (*Pause*) Look, if this is a touch, forget it! There's nothing doing! (*Another pause*) I try to forget the old days—I didn't like 'em! (*Annoyed*) You're just wasting your time! (*Another pause*) Jack, you're just wasting your time—and mine, too! Forget it!

Larry puts down the receiver and looks up to find Roy watching him

Roy Jack Keller?

Larry Yes. He's got one hell of a nerve trying to make a touch after all these years.

Roy I bumped into him about a week ago. He's a pathetic figure these days, I'm afraid.

Larry He always was a pathetic figure.

Roy (*with sentimental undertones*) Yes, I know, but—I've always had a soft spot for poor old Jack. When Dilys and I were first married, and living in those terrible digs in Maida Vale, he went out of his way to be kind to us.

Larry He's just a born loser, Roy. Forget him.

Roy Wasn't it Jack who first introduced you to Clare?

Larry (*nodding*) Yes, and the funny thing is she was crazy about him until I appeared on the scene. Heaven only knows what she saw in the guy.

Roy Well, he's really hit a new low now, poor devil. He's living on his own, over a pub in Shere Street.

Larry (*soft-pedalling*) Oh, I didn't realize that.

A tiny pause

Roy (*thoughtfully*) He gave you the first job you ever had.

Larry Yes, with the old Paternoster Agency. That seems a devil of a long time ago. What happened to that attractive wife of his?

Roy She died. (*A moment's pause*) I'm sorry you were rude to him, Larry. He's pretty desperate at the moment, I'm afraid.

Larry Yes, well, I didn't realize he was really up against it. I thought he was just trying it on. You know how it is. (*Taking hold of his brother's arm; smiling*) I'll tell you something about Jack Keller that'll amuse you. He's the only man who's ever really put the fear of the devil in me.

Roy (*surprised*) Jack?

Larry Yes. The poor devil thought I'd seduced his wife so one night he stuck a gun in my back, and threatened to shoot the living daylights out of me. Fortunately, his wife put in an appearance at the right psychological moment and we talked him out of it. But, believe me, it was a very nasty experience! (*Pleasantly, indicating the document*) Roy, I'll tell you what I think you ought to do about that. Take it home—read it again, quietly—and then show it to Dilys. Tell her what's in your mind and explain about the two hundred thousand dollars in my name in New York. Dilys is no fool. Listen to what she's got to say. If she says, "Go and see a lawyer", then it's O.K. by me, you go ahead and see one.

Roy (*somewhat relieved*) Yes, all right. Thank you, Larry. And please, don't think I don't appreciate what you've done, because I do. We all do.

Larry Sure, I realize that.

He moves with Roy towards the hall

I've got some presents for the children. Can I drop them in tomorrow morning?

Roy Yes, of course. Come and have breakfast with us.

Larry That's great. I'd like that.

Larry and Roy go out into the hall

Roy (*off*) Eight o'clock. Is that too early? We've got to get the kids off to school.

Larry (*off*) No. No, that's fine.

There is the sound of the door opening, off

(*Off*) See you tomorrow, Roy.

The door closes

Larry returns to the room and goes to the drinks cabinet

He no longer makes any attempt to conceal the fact that he is both annoyed and irritated. He is about to pour himself a drink when a sudden pain strikes him in the chest and he quickly grabs hold of the cabinet for support. Pause. Larry is obviously frightened, but gradually the pain subsides and he turns away from the cabinet and moves slowly down towards the sofa. He is now obviously feeling a great deal better and he gives an intense sigh of relief as he sinks on to the sofa. There is a long pause. The doorbell rings. He looks towards the hall. The bell rings again

He glances at his watch, hesitates, then rises and goes out into the hall. The front door opens

A Boy (*off*) Name of Campbell?
Larry (*off*) Yes.
A Boy (*off*) Telegram.
Larry (*off*) Thank you.

Larry comes back into the room and goes to the sofa, opening the telegram as he does so. The message obviously takes him by surprise and he stops dead in his tracks. It is several seconds before the full significance of the telegram dawns on him. Then, with an angry gesture and an unmistakable oath, he screws the telegram into a ball and tosses it across the the room towards the waste-paper basket

There is the sound of the front door opening and closing. Larry turns quickly

Clare Norman enters. Clare is attractive, tough, and at times very impetuous. She carries a newspaper and looks extremely angry

Larry Clare! (*He immediately takes her in his arms*)

Clare stands quite still, unresponsive. After a moment Larry releases her

What is it? What's the matter?
Clare (*indicating the newspaper*) Have you seen this?
Larry Of course I've seen it! (*He takes the paper from her, tosses it on to the sofa, and then takes her in his arms again*)

Clare struggles, trying to release herself, but after a little while she capitulates. Larry finally releases her and they stand facing each other. Clare glares at him, still intensely angry

Clare Why didn't you write?
Larry I did write.
Clare Two short letters and a stinking postcard! Did she tell you to send them?
Larry Who?
Clare (*angrily; pointing to the newspaper*) This girl—this Beth—whatever her name is!
Larry (*amused*) Clare—honey . . .
Clare Don't give me that honey routine! Dilys was right! She said you'd walk out on me!
Larry To hell with Dilys! (*Taking hold of her again*) Now, listen! And get this firmly planted in that empty little head of yours. I'm not walking out on anybody . . .
Clare Then what's all this crap? Who's this girl I've been reading about?

Larry Her name's Beth Sherman. Her father's one of the wealthiest men in America and for your information she's not, by any stretch of the imagination, a girl.

Clare Then what the hell is she—a performing seal?

Larry The description, curiously enough, is not entirely inapt.

Clare (*tensely, unable to control herself*) How old?

Larry What do you mean—how old?

Clare How old is she?

Larry She's an immature forty-five

Clare I don't believe you!

Larry All right, you don't believe me.

Clare (*still furious*) Beth Sherman! She sounds like something out of *Gone With the Wind*! I'll bet the little bitch is covered in mink.

Larry (*amused by her jealousy*) She prefers chinchilla.

Clare glares at him

Clare Are you going to marry her?

Larry Don't be ridiculous.

Clare Well—are you?

Larry Of course I'm not! I'm not going to marry anyone, unless you can persuade that righteous husband of yours to give you a divorce.

Clare (*gently; breaking away from him*) I'll tell you something. Something I didn't intend to tell you. While you were away I had time to think. For the very first time I was really honest with myself . . .

Larry About what?

Clare About us. I know now I'll never get you out of my system, Larry, however hard I try.

Larry Then why try?

Clare (*Shaking her head*) But I'm under no illusions. Not any longer. Just you remember that.

A tiny pause

Larry O.K., you've been frank with me. Now I'll be frank with you. So far as I'm concerned Beth Sherman is a pain in the neck. She means absolutely nothing to me! Less than nothing! But in order to get on the right side of her old man I just had to string along with her. Believe me, Clare, I had absolutely no choice in the matter.

Pause

Clare (*relenting slightly, with the first suggestion of a smile*) All right, I believe you. But . . .

Larry (*laughing*) Clare, for God's sake!

She laughs too, and he takes her in his arms again

Clare (*finally breaking away from him*) You said in your letter that you'd been ill.

Larry Yes, it was the old trouble. (*He taps his chest*) I had two attacks. One in New York and the other flying down to Chicago.

Clare Were they serious?

Larry No, not really. I've had worse.

Clare I suppose, as usual, you did nothing about it.

Larry As a matter of fact, I did. I saw a witch-doctor in New York. He charged me three hundred dollars, told me it was angina, which I already knew, and gave me some capsules.

Clare Did you take them?

Larry Well . . .

Clare Did you?

Larry Yes—off and on. I still take them occasionally. They relieve the pain, but—you know me, I hate taking things.

Clare Larry, you really are an idiot, neglecting your health the way you do.

Larry Yes, I know. I'll do something about it one of these days, I promise you.

Clare I wish you would. (*Looking at her watch*) I must fly, or I shall miss the recording!

Larry What time will you be finished?

Clare Oh—with a bit of luck, half-past ten.

Larry Well, let's have supper together. I'll see you at our usual restaurant at about eleven o'clock. How's that?

Clare Lovely, darling. (*She turns towards the hall, then stops*) When are you going back to New York?

Larry Well—I was hoping to go back at the weekend. I've got a meeting with Walter Sherman on Monday morning. Now, I don't know what's going to happen.

Clare What do you mean?

Larry I saw Roy just before you arrived. I wanted him to sign a contract; just a little agreement I'd drawn up. I was hoping to take it back to New York with me.

Clare Well?

Larry He refuses to sign it. Well—he didn't exactly refuse but he wants to talk to his lawyer about it.

Clare Is there any reason why he shouldn't talk to his lawyer?

Larry Of course there isn't! But you know lawyers! They can't see the wood for the trees! In the end, I was so damned annoyed, I told him to have a word with Dilys about it.

Clare Why did you do that?

Larry (*with a shrug*) It's a calculated risk. If Dilys says "sign it", he'll sign it.

Clare Yes, but supposing she doesn't?

Larry Then I'm in trouble.

Clare What sort of trouble?

Larry (*after a momentary hesitation*) Real trouble.

Clare looks at him

Clare (*quietly*) O.K., I've got the message. What is it you want me to do?

Larry Dilys likes you, Clare, she always has done. So I thought if you could possibly . . .

Clare (*interrupting him*) What is it you want me to do?

Larry I want you to talk to Dilys. Tell her that contract's got to be signed, and it's got to be signed within the next twenty-four hours. Tell her it's important, for Roy as well as me.

Clare (*sardonically*) For Roy as well as you?

Larry That's right.

There is a pause while they take each other in

Clare All right, you bastard. I'll phone her later, after the show.

Larry (*smiling, relieved*) Thank you, honey. (*With a sudden thought*) Wait a minute! I've got an idea! What about asking them to join us for supper?

Clare They'd never come. You know Dilys. Besides, there's always some confusion over baby-sitters.

Larry She'd come if you asked her, I'm sure she would.

Clare Well—I'll try. (*Kissing him*) Larry, I hate to rush away like this, but I really must go now!

Clare rushes out into the hall, followed by Larry

(*Off*) See you later, darling!

There is the sound of the front door opening and closing

Larry re-enters. He looks thoughtful but definitely happier. He puts out the main light and after switching on a small table lamp crosses to the alcove and turns on the television set. He moves the set so that the screen faces the easy chair and cannot be seen from the rest of the room. He adjusts the volume control and the sound of music fades in. He stands looking at the picture for a little while, faintly amused by what he sees, then he turns and goes into the bedroom

The music continues from the television set. There is a long pause

David slowly appears from the hall. He stands perfectly still, cautiously looking round the room. He is dressed in a dark suit and wears a glove on his right hand. He carries the gun in this hand. David is tense, but not nervous. He slowly comes into the room, then stops dead—obviously attracted by a noise from the bedroom. He watches the bedroom door, then quickly turns and moves back into the hall as Larry comes out of the bedroom wearing a dressing-gown

Larry picks up the newspaper from the settee, goes to the alcove, and sits in the easy chair. He looks at the television, undecided whether to watch the programme or read

David comes back into the room and moves slowly towards the alcove

As Larry leans forward to switch off the set David hesitates—tense, his eyes on the alcove. Larry's hand is on the television switch when he suddenly becomes aware that there is someone else in the room. He quickly rises; turning

Larry Who the devil . . . (*Astonished; moving down from the alcove*) Ryder! How the hell did you get in here?

David does not reply; he raises the gun until it is pointing at Larry. His hand is quite steady

Ryder! (*Tensely, frightened*) Ryder, for God's sake! Don't be a bloody fool! You'll never get away with it . . .

Larry suddenly stops speaking and gives a sharp cry, at the same time clutching his chest. It is obvious that he has had a recurrence of his heart trouble. He staggers towards the settee, now frightened by the increasing pain—almost unaware of David's presence. David watches him, obviously somewhat suspicious

(*Softly*) It's my heart . . .

The pain gradually increases and Larry sinks on to the settee, clutching his chest

There's some capsules in the bedroom—on the dressing-table . . .

David does not move. Larry's attack is obviously a severe one and as the pain becomes worse he lowers his head and clutches the arm of the settee

(*Weakly*)—Capsule—bedroom . . .

David still does not move. He looks highly suspicious as he stands, gun in hand, quietly staring down at Larry

The Lights fade to a Black-out. When Larry's room is completely dark, the Lights come up on David's room

It is eleven o'clock the next morning. Mrs Bedford has just finished cleaning the room and is now standing by the desk, telephone in hand

Mrs Bedford (*on the telephone*) . . . No, I'm sorry, he isn't here at the moment. Who is it calling? . . . Oh, good morning, Mr Foster! Mr Ryder's just slipped out to the post, he'll be back in a few minutes. Shall I ask him to give you a ring? . . . Oh, I see. Yes, certainly. . . . What's the message? I'll write it down. . . . (*She picks up a pen; as she listens her expression slowly changes. Pause*) When did this happen, sir? . . . No, I don't think so, in fact I'm sure he doesn't. . . . (*She puts the pen down*) Yes, of course! I'll tell him as soon as he comes in. . . . Is there any other message, Mr Foster? . . . Yes, I will.

Mrs Bedford replaces the receiver and stands for a moment or two obviously thinking about the telephone call

David enters

Mr Foster's just telephoned. He wanted to know if you'd heard about Mr Campbell.

David Larry Campbell?

Mrs Bedford Yes, sir. He's dead. Apparently he had a heart attack.

Pause

David When was this?

Mrs Bedford I think it was last night, sir.

Another pause

David Did Mr Foster say anything else?

Mrs Bedford Only that he'll be in touch with you later, sir, about the Norwich case.

David (*quietly, dismissing her*) Thank you, Mrs Bedford.

Mrs Bedford collects her vacuum cleaner and dusters and goes out

David remains quite still, deep in thought. Then, after a little while, he moves down to his desk and stands staring down at the photograph of his wife

There is a long pause—then Jo enters. She looks worried; there is a peculiar intensity about her

(*Pleased to see her*) Jo, my dear! I've just this minute posted you a letter! I felt so ashamed about last night, I simply had to write and apologize . . .

Jo Nonsense, David . . .

David I hope you weren't too embarrassed by my dashing backwards and forwards like that. It's this damn bug, I just don't seem to be able to get rid of it.

Jo (*who has not been listening to him*) I don't know whether you've heard or not—Larry Campbell's dead.

David Ernest telephoned a few minutes ago. I understand he had a heart attack.

Jo A heart attack? (*Shaking her head*) He was murdered.

David (*surprised*) Murdered?

Jo Yes. He was found in his bedroom, early this morning. There'd been a struggle.

David Good God! (*Suddenly, looking at her*) But who told you this? Where did you get this information from?

Jo I've just come from Scotland Yard. I've spent the best part of an hour with a man called Cleaver. He's in charge of the case.

David I know Inspector Cleaver. But what were you doing at Scotland Yard, Jo?

Jo I sent Larry a telegram. It had my name on it. The police found it so naturally they thought . . . David, I don't usually drink at this time of the morning but—do you think I could have a Scotch?

David looks at her

David Yes, of course, my dear.

While David gets the drink Jo goes and sits in the wing-chair. She takes a cigarette out of her handbag and is nervously trying to get her lighter to work when David rejoins her   .

   Here we are, Jo.
Jo Thank you.

Jo takes the glass and quickly drinks. David takes the lighter out of her hand and as she puts down the glass lights her cigarette for her. There is a brief, awkward silence

David Now what's all this about a telegram?
Jo Some little time ago a girl who worked for me—a very sweet girl— suddenly gave me notice. This was a bitter disappointment because, apart from losing a good secretary, I was terribly fond of the girl. The week she was due to leave I sent her a present and, rather unwisely as it turned out, wrote her several letters.
David What was in the letters?
Jo Nothing that I'm ashamed of. But they were very sentimental letters and I realize now that if someone deliberately quoted certain passages out of context . . . Well, you know what people are like. Especially the sort of people who read my column!
David Go on, Jo . . .
Jo About four months ago I had a phone call from Larry Campbell. He said he had the letters—God knows how he got hold of them— and that he was prepared to sell them to me for six thousand pounds. I said I'd think about it. (*She hesitates, and drinks*) Nothing happened for several weeks. I didn't hear another word from him. Then, yester- day morning, quite out of the blue, I received a telegram suggesting that we meet. At first I didn't know what to do. I thought of talking to you about it; asking your advice. Then I realized that you hadn't been well just recently and . . . Finally, I went to the bank and drew out the money.
David And then what did you do?
Jo (*hesitantly*) I sent Larry a telegram . . .
David Saying what?

Pause

Jo Drop dead.
David (*taken aback*) Drop dead!
Jo Yes. I then had a large Scotch, marched into Harrods, and bought myself a fur coat.

David looks at her, still somewhat surprised by her story, then with a faint smile he takes the empty glass out of her hand

David Did you tell the Inspector this?
Jo No, I didn't. I was going to tell him and then I thought—what the hell, he'll take one look at me and only believe half the story anyway. In the end, I told him Larry was trying to borrow some money from me.
David Did he believe you?

Jo I don't know. I hope he did. (*She rises. Pause. Not very convincingly*) I'm not worried, not unduly . . .

David (*quietly*) You look worried, Jo.

Jo Do I? (*She faces him*) Then you're the one I'm worried about.

David Me?

Jo Yes. Cleaver questioned me about last night. He wanted to know what my movements were. I told him we had dinner together. As soon as I mentioned your name he became interested. He started probing . . .

David Probing?

Jo Amongst other things he wanted to know about Evelyn and Larry and what happened in the South of France.

David Did you tell him what happened?

Jo No. But I have a feeling he already knew.

David (*quietly*) I see. (*Thoughtfully*) Thank you, Jo. Thank you for telling me this. (*He slowly turns away from her*)

Mrs Bedford enters

Mrs Bedford There's a gentleman to see you, sir. He says his name's Cleaver. He's a police officer.

Jo looks at David

David Ask him to come in.

Mrs Bedford goes

Jo Do you mind if I stay, David?

David No, I don't mind. But haven't you had enough of Mr Cleaver for one morning?

Jo (*after a slight hesitation*) I'd like to stay, if you've no objection.

David No, of course not. Stay by all means.

John Cleaver enters. He carries an attaché case

Cleaver Mr Ryder? Chief-Inspector Cleaver. (*To Jo, pleasantly*) Hello, Miss Mitchell.

Jo nods

We've met before, sir.

David (*shaking hands*) That's right. I'm just trying to remember where, exactly.

Cleaver (*taking stock of the room*) Burton-on-Trent. Company director. Embezzlement case.

David Yes, of course! I remember now. Do sit down.

Cleaver Thank you, sir. (*He moves to the sofa*) Mr Ryder, I imagine Miss Mitchell has already told you that I'm making inquiries about a man called Larry Campbell.

David Yes.

Cleaver He was found murdered, early this morning. Brutally murdered.

David makes no comment

Naturally we've already started questioning Mr Campbell's friends and acquaintances and on more than one occasion, sir, your name has been mentioned.

David My name?

Cleaver Well—perhaps I should have said your wife's name.

David My wife's dead, Inspector.

Cleaver Yes, I realize that, sir, but . . .

David What is it you want to know about my wife?

Cleaver How well did she know Mr Campbell?

David (*bluntly*) She had an affair with him.

Cleaver You mean your wife left you, and went off with Mr Campbell?

David That's precisely what I mean.

Cleaver (*nodding*) That's more or less what I'd heard, sir. I suppose you wouldn't like to tell me the rest of the story?

David My wife met Campbell and became infatuated with him. Not, I might add, an unusual turn of events so far as Mr Campbell was concerned.

Cleaver No, I gather he was something of a womanizer.

David They went down to the South of France together. Whilst they were there my wife became ill and was rushed into hospital. She died.

Cleaver Is that the complete story?

David Yes—more or less.

Cleaver Correct me if I'm mistaken, sir, but wasn't your son killed in a car accident on the way to the hospital?

David Yes, he was. But that had nothing to do with Campbell.

Cleaver No, sir? (*A moment's pause*) I was given to understand by a friend of yours that there was quite a scene when you arrived at the hospital.

David Yes, I'm afraid there was. By the time I got there my wife was dead. I was desperate. Overwrought. I threatened to kill Campbell.

Cleaver Was Mr Campbell present when you made the threat?

David No, he wasn't. If he had have been you wouldn't be here now, Inspector.

Cleaver What does that mean, sir?

David It means I would have killed him.

A slight pause

Cleaver Well, thank you for being so frank, Mr Ryder. Now perhaps you'll be equally frank about what happened last night.

David Last night?

Cleaver Yes, I believe you and Miss Mitchell had dinner together.

David That's correct. We went to the Hilton.

Cleaver Miss Mitchell tells me you arrived at the hotel at about seven o'clock and left at approximately a quarter to eleven.

Jo (*to David*) It was about a quarter to eleven, wasn't it?

David Yes, I think so. We spent quite some time in the bar with Ernest. (*To Cleaver*) That's Ernest Foster, a friend of mine.

Cleaver (*nodding*) Yes, I know, sir. I've already spoken to Mr Foster.

David (*surprised*) Indeed?

Cleaver I understand you were not feeling too good, sir, and during the course of the evening had to leave the table several times.

David Yes, that's true. I've had some sort of a tummy bug; I just don't seem to be able to get rid of it.

Cleaver Where did you go when you left the table, sir?

David Where did I go? Where the devil do you think I went? I went to the lavatory, of course.

Cleaver (*unperturbed*) Which one? There are several, sir. One near the restaurant, one on the ground floor, and another one . . .

David I had the dubious pleasure of being a frequent visitor to both. If I hadn't been with Miss Mitchell I should have jumped into a cab and come straight home.

Cleaver I can't imagine why you didn't.

David I didn't for the simple reason that I didn't want to disappoint Miss Mitchell. I'd already done that once—I made a date with her last week and forgot all about it—and I didn't wish to disappoint her again.

Cleaver Do you often go to the Hilton, sir?

David No, not often.

Cleaver Then why choose that particular restaurant last night?

Jo looks at David, obviously recalling her earlier comment about the choice of restaurant

David I'd heard very good reports of it, so I thought we'd try it.

Cleaver I see. So you had, in fact, no ulterior motive?

David What possible ulterior motive could I have had?

Cleaver Mr Campbell's flat is very near the Hilton, sir.

David Is it? I wouldn't know about that.

Cleaver This morning I made a point of walking from the flat to the main entrance of the hotel. I walked quite slowly, Mr Ryder. It took me exactly four minutes and fifty-five seconds.

Jo What are you suggesting, Inspector?

Cleaver (*quietly*) I think Mr Ryder knows what I'm suggesting. (*To David*) I'm suggesting that you kept your appointment, sir.

David *What* appointment?

Cleaver Your appointment with Mr Campbell.

David (*amazed*) My appointment with Mr Campbell?

Cleaver Yes, sir. (*A moment's pause*) Mr Ryder, why do you think I came to see you this morning?

David You told me why! You'd heard that my wife was a friend of Campbell's.

Cleaver That wasn't the only reason.

Jo What was the other reason, Inspector?

Cleaver Mr Ryder made an appointment to see Larry Campbell. The appointment was for nine o'clock last night.

David But that's not true! It's just not true!

David looks across at Jo, obviously bewildered

Jo Suppose you put us in the picture, Inspector, and tell us exactly what happened last night?

Cleaver Campbell arrived from the States yesterday morning. His girl-friend—Clare Norman—was rehearsing all day and she didn't see him until about eight o'clock. They arranged to have supper together later in the evening. Miss Norman arrived at the restaurant at a quarter past eleven. There was no sign of Larry. She waited until midnight and when he didn't show up she decided to go home. When Miss Norman arrived at the flat she found the front door unlocked and partly open. She also found Larry Campbell's body in the bedroom. There'd obviously been a struggle; his clothes were torn and he was covered in blood.

Cleaver pauses, takes a piece of paper out of his pocket, and looks at David who has been listening intently to what he has been saying

She found this note on the pad by the telephone. (*Reading the note*) "Nine o'clock. Ryder."

Jo (*staggered*) Did Larry write that?

Cleaver Yes, he did.

David But he couldn't have done!

Cleaver Why not?

David Because I didn't have an appointment with him.

Cleaver (*looking at the note again*) Then why write this, sir? And he did write it—make no mistake about that! Our handwriting experts have examined the note and compared it with letters written by Mr Campbell. He wrote this, sir—and it's pretty obvious he wrote it immediately after receiving a telephone call.

David Well, the call wasn't from me, Inspector! I made no appointment to see Larry Campbell, or anyone else, last night.

Cleaver I see.

Jo At what time was the murder committed, do you know?

Cleaver Some time after eight, and not later than half past eleven.

David While I was at the Hilton, or on the way home, in fact.

Cleaver (*hesitantly*) Yes, sir.

David (*with a note of sarcasm*) Providing, of course, you accept the fact that I was at the Hilton.

Cleaver I accept the fact that you arrived there at seven o'clock and left at a quarter to eleven. But I'm not convinced that you stayed there the whole evening, sir.

David Why not?

Cleaver (*after a moment*) Your story's a little too vague for my liking. You take Miss Mitchell out to dinner and suddenly don't feel very well, so——

David (*interrupting him*) It wasn't a question of *suddenly* not feeling well. I haven't been feeling well for some little time.

Jo That's true, Inspector.

Cleaver (*with a nod*) All right. You didn't feel very well so you went to the cloakroom.

David (*irritated*) The lavatory . . .

Cleaver The lavatory. During the course of the evening you visited the lavatory at least three times if my information's correct.

David I'm sure it is, Inspector.

Cleaver And not always the same one, either, sir. Now why was that?

David (*with a shrug*) I just didn't want to be seen going backwards and forwards to the same place.

Cleaver It's made it much more difficult for us to check your story, sir.

David Well—that's unfortunate.

Cleaver Not from your point of view, Mr Ryder. Indeed, if you'd planned the whole thing, quite deliberately, it couldn't have worked out better from your point of view.

Jo looks at David

However, the point is, on one occasion you left Miss Mitchell for at least a quarter of an hour.

David Yes.

Cleaver (*faintly surprised*) You admit it was a quarter of an hour, sir?

David (*irritated*) Yes, of course! It may have been half-an-hour, for all I know!

Cleaver (*politely*) I don't think it could have been half-an-hour, sir.

The telephone rings and, still looking at Cleaver, David crosses and picks up the receiver. Jo turns her back on Cleaver. She is obviously worried

David (*on the telephone*) Hello? . . . Speaking. . . . Yes, he is—just a moment. (*To Cleaver*) It's for you . . .

Cleaver moves down and takes the receiver. David looks across at Jo. He realizes that she is perturbed and greatly puzzled

Cleaver (*on the telephone*) Cleaver speaking. . . . Oh, hello, Sergeant! . . . No, that's all right. . . . Yes, but go ahead. . . . (*Trying to conceal a note of surprise*) When? . . .

David and Jo look across at Cleaver, obviously attracted by his tone of voice

(*Cautiously*) Where are you speaking from? . . . No, don't do that, stay where you are. . . . Yes. . . . Yes, I will, immediately. . . . (*He replaces the receiver, nods to David, and after picking up his attaché case moves towards the doorway*) If you'll excuse me, sir.

David (*curiously*) What's happened, Inspector?

Cleaver (*after hesitating*) There's been a new development. (*To Jo*) Goodbye, Miss Mitchell. Thank you, once again, for your help.

Cleaver looks at David, makes as if to say something, then changes his mind and goes out. David follows him

Jo crosses to the desk and thoughtfully stubs her cigarette out in the ashtray

David returns

Jo (*turning; quietly*) What happened last night?

David does not answer. They look at each other, steadily

You've got to tell me!

David I went to Campbell's flat. I intended to kill him and—make it look like suicide.

Jo (*alarmed*) Oh, David . . .

David But I didn't kill him! I swear I didn't!

Jo Then what happened?

David He had a heart attack and—well, God knows why—I changed my mind.

Jo (*softly, desperately worried*) David, I can't believe this—I don't believe it——

David (*tensely, interrupting her*) I knew what I was doing, Jo! Don't try and make excuses for me—I knew exactly what I was doing. (*A tiny pause*) One night, not long after Jonathan was killed, I saw Campbell. He was standing in a doorway. There was a girl with him. They were laughing and talking, both obviously amused by something. For days I couldn't get that picture out of my mind. I kept telling myself that he'd seen me and that he'd said something to the girl, something malicious about Evelyn. I knew it wasn't true. My instinct told me it wasn't true and yet—I wanted to believe it, Jo. I had to believe it, because I'd made up my mind to kill him!

Jo But how did you get into the flat?

David A man called George Rudd made a key for me. I invented a story about a divorce case and my wanting to get hold of some photographs . . .

Jo But don't you realize the moment he hears about the murder . . .

David Rudd's in Canada. I paid his fare. That was my part of the bargain.

Jo (*hesitantly*) Is this the truth, David?

David Yes, I swear it is!

Jo (*still puzzled*) But if you had a key to the flat, why make an appointment to see Larry?

David But I didn't! That's what I don't understand!

Jo Then how do you explain the note, by the telephone?

David There's only one possible explanation. (*He looks at her*) Someone telephoned Larry, and pretended to be me.

Mrs Bedford enters

Mrs Bedford I'm sorry to trouble you, sir, but that young man's here again.

David Young man?

Rudd appears from the hall. He wears a raincoat and stands, smiling, looking down at Mrs Bedford

(*After a moment, quietly*) That's all right, Mrs Bedford.

Mrs Bedford turns, looks at Rudd, then goes out

Rudd Good morning, Mr Ryder . . .

A pause

David Hello, Rudd. (*Quietly*) This is a surprise . . .

Rudd Yes, I thought it would be. I nearly phoned you this morning and then I thought—well, it's better if I pop round and see Mr Ryder.

David Did you miss the plane?

Rudd No, I didn't miss it exactly. I just wasn't able to get away.

David Why not?

Rudd (*looking at Jo*) Oh, one or two things went wrong. There was a bit of a mix-up. You know how it is.

David No, I'm afraid I don't.

Rudd Well . . . (*He still looks at Jo*)

David This is Miss Mitchell—she's a friend of mine. (*Nodding*) It's all right, Rudd.

Rudd Yes, well, I've got one or two things I'd like to talk to you about, Mr Ryder. They're a bit on the personal side, so perhaps . . . (*He continues looking at Jo*)

David That's all right. Go ahead.

Jo (*moving towards the door*) I'll see you later, David.

David No, Jo, please!

Jo It's all right, David. I want to have a word with Mrs Bedford.

Jo goes out

David (*annoyed*) Now, what is it you want?

Rudd Well, at the moment I could do with a drink.

David Rudd, I'm entertaining Miss Mitchell. If you've got anything to say, please say it!

Rudd Righto! (*After a moment, facing him*) Did you do it?

David Do what?

Rudd You know what I'm talking about. The murder. Did you do it?

David I fail to see what business it is of yours whether . . .

Rudd (*interrupting him*) Look, Mr Ryder, I made that key. If you hadn't had the key you couldn't have got into the flat.

David What's that got to do with it?

Rudd It's got a hell of a lot to do with it! That key incriminates me. Puts the finger on me good and proper. Surely, you don't need me to tell you that.

David (*curtly*) The key doesn't incriminate anyone—for the simple reason that I didn't use it!

Rudd (*scornfully*) Don't give me that! You used it all right.

David (*quietly, watching him*) How do you know?

Rudd I saw you.

David When?

Rudd Last night.

David (*quietly*) Go on, Rudd.

Rudd What do you mean—go on?

David Tell me more. I'm interested.

Rudd (*after a moment; rather pleased with himself*) O.K. I didn't believe that tale of yours about the divorce case. I knew you was up to something, so I watched the flat. I watched it all night. I saw you go in and I saw you come out.

David What does that prove? (*He shrugs*) Simply that I was searching for the photographs I wanted.

Rudd But you just said you didn't use the key. (*He sits on the arm of a chair*) You'd better make your mind up. Mr Ryder.

David looks at Rudd. There is a long pause

David Yes, I think I'd better. (*Quite friendly*) You said you wanted a drink?

Rudd Well, I could certainly do with one.

David turns and crosses to the drinks trolley

David (*mixing Rudd a whisky and soda*) I take it I underrated you, Rudd, and you hadn't the slightest intention of emigrating.

Rudd Oh, I wouldn't say that. (*Smiling*) It was me that underrated you, Mr Ryder. I expected the money, not the ticket.

David (*bringing the drink down to Rudd*) Let's just say we underrated each other.

Rudd (*taking the drink*) Thanks. (*He drinks*) Mr Ryder, I've got a friend who's opening a sauna parlour on the King's Road. He wants me to join him. Offered to make me a partner, in fact. (*He drinks again, and looks at the glass*) The trouble is I've got to find five thousand quid from somewhere. It's not a lot of money, of course, but—it is if you haven't got it.

David And you haven't got it?

Rudd You know I haven't.

David Go on, Rudd.

Rudd Well, I did you a favour—getting you the key, I mean—and I don't think I was particularly well paid for it.

David Don't you, Rudd?

Rudd No, I don't. Now I don't want you to get the wrong impression— this isn't blackmail.

David I'm relieved to hear it.

Rudd On the other hand, if I was to tell the police that you went to that flat last night, you and that solicitor friend of yours . . .

David (*puzzled*) Solicitor friend of mine?

Rudd You know who I mean—Foster.

David What are you talking about?

Rudd (*after a moment*) You've underrated me once, don't do it again, there's a good chap.

David You—saw Mr Foster last night?

Rudd 'Course I did! He went to Campbell's flat.

David When?

Rudd Come off it!

David (*quietly, yet with authority*) When did he go to the flat?

Rudd Oh, some time after you left. Must have been about half-past ten. (*Watching David*) Don't tell me you didn't know. (*Smiling*) Do you know what I think? I think you and Foster are in this thing together, whatever it is. I think you knocked off Campbell and then he turned up later and went through the flat.

David Why should he do that?

Rudd I don't know why—perhaps you forgot something. (*With a shrug*) Perhaps I'm wrong and those photographs do exist.

A pause

David Where were you, Rudd—in a car?

Rudd (*nodding*) Yes.

David I didn't see you.

Rudd (*smiling*) I didn't intend you to.

A pause

David Supposing I told you I hadn't got five thousand pounds?

Rudd Then I should tell you to get it!

David And where do you propose I get it from?

Rudd (*smiling*) That's up to you. But if I were in your shoes I should try Mr Foster.

David And supposing Foster hasn't got it?

Rudd My word, you do look on the black side, don't you? You'll get it. (*Looking round the room, smiling*) You'll get it all right. Not to worry.

David Yes, but supposing I don't?

Rudd (*the smile fading*) Then I shall have to make an anonymous phone call to the police.

David (*quietly, quite politely*) And you don't call that blackmail?

Rudd (*a shade uncomfortably*) No, I don't. You owe me five thousand quid—that's how I look at it.

David Yes, well unfortunately for you, that's not how I look at it. (*He goes to the desk*) However, let's be fair. There's two sides to every question. (*Picking up the telephone*) You don't think this is blackmail. I do. So let's get a second opinion, shall we? (*He starts to dial*)

Rudd (*moving closer to him*) Who are you phoning?

David looks at Rudd. He does not answer. There is a pause. The number is ringing out

(*Moving nearer; tensely*) You heard what I said!

David (*suddenly, into the telephone*) Scotland Yard? Put me through to Chief-Inspector Cleaver. . . . Thank you. . . .

Rudd (*with an uneasy little laugh*) You can't kid me! You're bluffing!

David (*offering Rudd the receiver*) Here we are. Talk to him yourself . . .

Rudd takes the receiver, hesitates, then suddenly panics and quickly replaces it. He turns on David

Rudd You bugger! What do you think you're playing at?

David Let me give you a piece of advice, Rudd—based on personal experience. Don't get out of your depth.

Rudd is about to retort as—

Jo enters, followed by Ernest. Ernest wears outdoor clothes and carries a briefcase

Jo (*to David*) I'm sorry, David, but Ernest wants to see you.

David (*quietly, looking at Rudd*) That's all right, Jo. Mr Rudd's just leaving.

Rudd stares at David, then across at Ernest. He is angry and uncertain, both of himself and his next move. Finally he forces a smile

Rudd I'll keep in touch, Mr Ryder.

Rudd gives a little nod and goes out, watched by Ernest and Jo

Ernest (*to David, puzzled*) Is that young man still trying to borrow money from you?

David Yes, I'm afraid he is.

Ernest (*still looking after Rudd*) I wouldn't trust him an inch.

Jo (*to David*) Ernest wants to talk to you. He saw Larry Campbell last night.

Ernest (*correcting her, a shade irritated*) No, I didn't see him, Jo! I spoke to him on the phone.

Jo But I thought you said you went to his flat?

Ernest Yes, I did, but he was out—at least, there was no reply.

David I didn't realize you knew Campbell?

Ernest I didn't know him. But his brother, Roy, is a client of mine and he dropped in on me last night. (*He hesitates*) I'd better tell you what happened. Roy said his brother had just returned from America and had given him a contract to sign which he wasn't very happy about. I took a quick look at the document and, to say the least, I wasn't very happy about it either. After Roy left I took it on myself to telephone Larry . . .

Jo What time would that be?

Ernest About nine o'clock. I fully expected him to be difficult, but to my surprise he wasn't. On the contrary, he simply oozed charm. In the end he suggested we had a drink together and discuss the contract. He gave me his address, which is quite near where I live, and I strolled round there at about—ten-thirty. When I got to the flat there was no reply. I rang the bell, knocked on the door several times, but nothing happened. In the end I gave it up as a bad job and went back home.

David Have you told the police about this?

Ernest Yes, I told Inspector Cleaver. He was waiting for me when I arrived at the office this morning. From what he said I thought someone had simply broken into Larry's flat and he'd taken fright and had a heart attack. (*Looking at Jo*) But I gather from Jo that's not what happened?

David No, apparently not. But tell me: why should Cleaver call on you, Ernest?

Ernest He was checking up on Roy Campbell's story. He'd already seen Roy and been told about the contract.

David I see. (*A moment's pause*) Was my name mentioned, by any chance?

Ernest By Cleaver? Yes, it was. He asked me if I was a friend of yours. When I said I was he started asking me questions about your wife and her association with Larry Campbell.

David And what did you say?

Ernest What do you think I said? I said so far as that particular story was concerned you were by far and away the most reliable source of information.

David Thank you, Ernest.

Ernest Now if you'll excuse me. (*He looks at his watch*) I'm seeing the Norwich people this afternoon and, if I remember rightly, you said you'd made a few notes which might be of help to us.

David Yes, I have.

David goes to the desk and gets a folder from one of the drawers. He glances at it, then hands it to Ernest

Ernest Thank you. It's very good of you, David. (*He puts the folder in his case*) I'll read them on the train. Good-bye, Jo!

Jo Good-bye, Ernest.

Ernest, accompanied by David, moves towards the hall

Ernest You know, if the police are looking for a suspect, they haven't far to look. Roy Campbell had a first-class motive. That brother of his was really pulling a fast one.

Ernest goes out, followed by David. After a moment David returns

Jo (*quietly*) What did Rudd want?

David He tried to blackmail me.

Jo What happened?

David I called his bluff—but I'm very much afraid I haven't heard the last of Mr Rudd. He was watching the flat last night. He saw Ernest as well as me.

Jo Ernest said he phoned Larry about nine o'clock. Was that after you left?

David Yes, I was back at the hotel by twenty-to-nine.

Jo So if Ernest was telling the truth, Larry was alive and well enough to take a phone call, half an hour or so after you left him!

David Yes. Then when was he killed? And how did the man—if it was a man—get into the flat?

Jo Perhaps Larry let him in. Perhaps it was someone he knew; someone he was expecting.

David According to the note Clare Norman found he was expecting me. (*A tiny pause*) Jo, have you ever met this girl?

Jo Clare Norman? Yes, I have.

David What's she like?

Jo Blonde. Attractive. I imagine she could be pretty ruthless if she wanted to be. I met her about six months ago when I was doing an article on a musical show.

David Is she married?

Jo Yes; she's separated from her husband. He's a housemaster at a public school, somewhere up North. (*Thoughtfully; moving down to him*) David, you said just now that Rudd was watching the flat, that he saw both you and Ernest.

David Yes.

Jo Ernest arrived at the flat at about ten-thirty and got no reply.

David That's right.

Jo Let's assume he got no reply *not* because Larry was out, but because he was already dead.

David (*curiously*) What are you getting at, Jo?

Jo (*after a moment*) I'm getting at this. If Rudd was still watching the flat when Ernest arrived—and Larry was already dead—then Rudd must have seen the murderer.

David Yes—yes, he must have done.

Voices are heard. Jo and David look towards the hall

Cleaver enters, followed by Mrs Bedford. The Inspector looks serious and still carries his attaché case

Cleaver I'd like a word with you, Mr Ryder. It's important, sir.

David Yes, of course. Come in, Inspector. (*He nods to Mrs Bedford*)

Mrs Bedford exits

Cleaver looks at David, then at Jo; finally he puts the attaché case down on the arm of the sofa. He opens the case and takes out a cloth which conceals a fairly heavy object. He carefully unwraps the cloth, revealing the bronze figure

Cleaver (*after a moment*) Have you seen this before, sir?

David (*staring at the statuette*) Why—no . . .

Cleaver Are you sure?

David Of course I'm sure! What is it?

Cleaver It's a statuette, sir . . .

David I can see that!

Jo Isn't it Aprhodite, the Goddess of Love?

Cleaver (*looking at the statuette*) The Goddess of Love? I wouldn't know about that, Miss Mitchell. (*He looks up*) It's the weapon that killed Larry Campbell. (*He turns towards David*) It was missing from his bedroom. We've been searching for it since one o'clock this morning.

David I'm glad you found it, Inspector.

A tiny pause

Cleaver So am I, sir. (*He looks at David*) It was in the boot of your car.

With his eyes still on David the Inspector wraps the figure in the cloth again and returns it to the attaché case

The Lights fade to a Black-out, as—

the CURTAIN *falls*

ACT II

The same. Forty-eight hours later

The Lights slowly rise on Larry Campbell's flat. Clare Norman is discovered sitting on the floor, surrounded by a mass of letters and receipts. She is examining these in a perfunctory manner and placing them in a drawer by her side. Clare wears a dark dress and appears tense and restless. Roy Campbell's hat and coat are on the back of the settee. Clare finally rises, picks up the drawer and places it on the table. Roy comes out of the bedroom carrying a large brown paper parcel

Roy The wardrobe's empty and I've been through most of the cupboards. (*He goes to the table and puts down the parcel*)

Clare Oh, thank you, Roy. You've been a great help—both you and Dilys. I don't honestly know what I should have done without you both.

Roy (*moving towards her*) Don't be silly! What did you expect us to do, after all you've been through? My God, Clare—no-one realizes more than I do what a dreadful experience it must have been. But you've really got to try and pull yourself together. Please, Clare!

Clare (*nodding, with a suggestion of a smile*) Yes, all right.

Roy Now the best thing you can do is pack a bag and come and stay with us for two or three days.

Clare No—it's awfully kind of you, and I appreciate it. (*Shaking her head, a shade tense*) But I don't want to do that—not now, not today.

Roy That's just being stupid! It doesn't make any difference to us, you know. We can easily move the kids into one room.

Clare No, please, Roy! I'd rather stay here for the time being!

The doorbell rings. Roy turns and looks towards the hall

Roy Are you expecting someone?

Clare No.

Clare hesitates, then goes out into the hall. After a moment we hear the front door open and the sound of voices

Cleaver (*off*) Good morning, Miss Norman. Is Mr Campbell with you, by any chance?

Clare (*off; surprised*) Why, yes . . .

Cleaver (*off*) Do you think I might have a word with him?

Clare (*off*) Yes, certainly. Come along in, Inspector!

Roy crosses to the settee and picks up his hat and coat

Cleaver enters, followed by Clare

Cleaver (*to Roy, pleasantly*) Good morning, Mr Campbell, I called at your

house but apparently we just missed each other. Your wife said you
might be here.

Roy I'm just leaving.

Cleaver Perhaps you can spare me a moment or two, sir?

Roy (*nervously*) Yes, if it's important.

Clare moves towards the bedroom door, but Roy stops her

(*To Clare*) I'd like you to stay, Clare.

Cleaver I'd like Miss Norman to stay, too. (*Smiling at Clare*) She might
be able to help us.

Clare indicates the armchair near the table

Clare Sit down, Inspector.

*Clare sits and Cleaver crosses and takes the armchair, glancing down at the
brown paper parcel as he does so*

Cleaver Mr Campbell, when I last spoke to you, you told me that you'd
always been on friendly terms with your brother.

Roy Yes . . .

Cleaver You also told me that the last time you saw him he suddenly
produced a document which he wanted you to sign.

Roy (*a shade nervously*) Yes, that's right.

Cleaver Were you satisfied with the document, sir?

Roy More or less.

Cleaver What does that mean?

Clare It means *he* was satisfied with it, but his wife wasn't. That's true,
isn't it, Roy?

Roy (*tonelessly*) Yes, I suppose so.

Cleaver Your solicitor showed me a copy of the document. I don't think
I'd have been very satisfied with it, sir, if I'd been in your shoes.

Clare (*sharply*) What are you getting at?

Cleaver (*politely*) Getting at?

Clare What are you trying to prove? That Roy quarrelled with Larry?

Cleaver (*to Roy, pleasantly*) Did you quarrel with your brother?

Roy No, I didn't. I wasn't too happy with the agreement but I daresay
I'd have signed it, but for what Dilys said.

Cleaver What did your wife say, sir?

Roy (*with a nervous glance towards Clare*) She said you can trust your
friends but you can't always trust your relatives.

Cleaver And that's why you consulted Mr Foster, because of what your
wife said?

Roy Well—yes. (*After a moment; wishing to close the interview*) Was that
why you wanted to see me, Inspector?

Cleaver Partly, sir. I also wanted to ask you about a man called Jack
Keller. I take it you've heard of Mr Keller?

Roy (*puzzled*) Why, yes . . .

Cleaver Is he a friend of yours?

Roy He used to be, but I haven't seen him for ages. (*Suddenly*) No, that's
not true, I bumped into him about ten days ago. We all used to work for

the same advertizing agency. Larry, Jack and I. Then Jack started up
on his own and went bust, poor devil.

Cleaver I understand he had a very attractive wife?

Roy Yes, he had.

Cleaver Did your brother ever hear from Mr Keller?

Roy looks at Cleaver, obviously surprised by the question

Roy He telephoned Larry on Monday and tried to borrow some money
from him.

Cleaver Was he successful?

Roy No, he wasn't. Larry was rather rude to him, I'm afraid.

Cleaver (*after a moment's thought, pleasantly dismissing him*) Well, thank
you, Mr Campbell, that's all I wanted to know. Sorry to have detained
you.

Roy (*a shade surprised*) Oh—that's all right! (*He hesitates, then puts on
his hat and coat and picks up the brown paper parcel*) I shall be at home if
you want me, Clare.

Roy nods to Cleaver and goes out into the hall

A pause

Clare (*puzzled and curious*) Why are you interested in this man—Jack
Keller?

Cleaver His wife was a good-looking woman and Larry Campbell tried
to seduce her. Her husband heard about it and threatened to murder
him.

Clare (*angrily*) Who told you that nonsense?

Cleaver (*looking at her, ignoring her remark*) Miss Norman, I expect this
is the first time you've been involved in a murder case?

Clare I try not to make a habit of it.

Cleaver Well, I've had the dubious pleasure of investigating half a dozen,
and invariably I've found myself up against the same problem. Someone
—not necessarily the murderer—refuses to tell me the truth.

Clare Are you suggesting that I'm not telling you the truth?

Cleaver I'm suggesting that when I first questioned you, you deliberately
gave me a false account of your meeting with Campbell.

Clare That's not true! I told you exactly what transpired between us.

Cleaver You told me Mr Campbell was delighted to see you and you were
delighted to see him.

Clare Well?

Cleaver You gave me the impression you fell into each other's arms and
there were soft lights and sweet music.

Clare (*annoyed*) So?

Cleaver I don't believe that.

Clare Why don't you believe it?

Cleaver (*pleasantly*) Miss Norman, don't be deceived by my somewhat
boyish appearance. I've been around. I read books. I've even met a
few women in my time. (*After a moment, looking at her*) It's my bet you

played hell with him on Monday night. It's my bet you read about this American girl, Beth Sherman, and you really went to town on Mr Campbell. Am I right?

A pause

Clare (*quietly*) Yes.

Cleaver (*not unpleasantly*) Why on earth didn't you tell me that in the first place? Now what exactly happened between you?

Clare (*after a moment*) I accused Larry of having an affair with Beth whatever-her-name-is. He denied it and we had a row. Finally he convinced me that there was nothing in it—at least nothing for me to worry about—and we—well, we made it up.

Cleaver (*quietly*) Go on.

Clare We arranged to have supper together and I went back to the BBC.

Cleaver What time was that?

Clare I told you. About eight-fifteen. As soon as I arrived at the studio I telephoned Dilys—Mrs Campbell. Larry wanted me to talk to her about the contract. He thought if the four of us had supper together it might, well . . .

Cleaver Ease the situation?

Clare (*nodding*) Unfortunately Dilys made it quite clear that neither she, nor Roy, had the slightest intention of having supper with us.

Cleaver I see. (*After a moment, thoughtfully*) Miss Norman, did Mr Campbell—Larry, that is—ever mention David Ryder to you?

Clare He told me about his affair with Mrs Ryder, if that's what you mean.

Cleaver You know that Ryder threatened to murder him on one occasion?

Clare nods

Did anyone else ever threaten Mr Campbell?

Clare Not that I'm aware of.

Cleaver Except Jack Keller, of course.

Clare (*turning away from him*) I don't know anything about Jack Keller.

Cleaver But surely, you knew him?

Clare Yes, I knew him. Vaguely.

Cleaver Vaguely, Miss Norman?

Clare (*still not looking at him*) Yes, vaguely. He was never a close friend of mine.

Cleaver But, as I understand it, it was Jack Keller who introduced you to Mr Campbell.

Clare Was it? I don't remember . . .

A tiny pause

Cleaver How long had you and Mr Campbell been living together?

Clare About six months.

Cleaver Was there ever any question of your getting married?

Clare Yes. We wanted to get married but my husband wouldn't divorce me.

Cleaver Why not?

Clare (*irritated*) I don't know why not, Inspector. I wish to God I did.

Cleaver Does your husband work in London?

Clare No, he's a housemaster at a school near Darlington. But if you take my advice you won't waste five minutes on my husband. He's in love with the first eleven. I doubt whether he knew Larry existed.

Cleaver (*smiling*) Thank you, Miss Norman. (*He picks up his hat*)

Clare moves towards the hall with him

Please don't bother, I can let myself out.

He goes. Clare stands looking towards the hall, then, as she hears the front door close, she picks up the drawer containing the letters etc., and goes into the bedroom. After a little while she returns from the bedroom carrying a cardboard box. Now that Cleaver has departed she looks more relaxed; she has taken off her dress and is now simply wearing pants and a bra

She crosses to the drinks cabinet and, taking a knife out of one of the drawers, cuts the string which is holding the box together. She puts the knife down on the cabinet and removes the lid of the box. The box contains a brightly coloured negligée and a pair of matching mules. Clare slips into the negligée and puts on the mules. She is quietly admiring herself when the doorbell rings. Somewhat taken by surprise, she looks towards the hall. The bell rings again. Clare hesitates, then quickly collects the cardboard box and the loose string and tosses them through the open door of the bedroom

She takes a deep breath, adjusts the negligée, and goes calmly out into the hall. We hear the front door open

Rudd (*off*) Good afternoon. I'm from the National Assurance Company. I've called about a policy of Mr Campbell's—Mr Larry Campbell.

Clare (*off*) Yes?

Rudd (*off*) I take it I've got the right address?

Clare (*off*) This is Mr Campbell's flat.

Rudd (*off*) Then may I come in?

Rudd appears from the hall, followed by Clare

Clare (*puzzled*) What did you say your name was?

Rudd ignores the question. He is looking round the room

Rudd (*turning, after a moment*) Pardon?

Clare I asked what your name was?

Rudd It's Rudd. George Rudd. (*He looks at her, notices the negligée, and likes what he sees*) I've seen you before somewhere, haven't I?

Clare It's possible.

Rudd (*suddenly realizing*) I've seen you on the box! In the Billy West Show.

Clare Yes, I've been in several of them.

Rudd And very good you were, too. (*He looks at her*) Very good indeed, if I may say so. But he's a bit of a pain, isn't he?

Clare (*puzzled by his manner*) You say you're from the National Assurance Company?

Rudd That's right.

Clare Which branch?

Rudd (*glibly*) City Branch. Throgmorton Street.

Clare Well, what is it you want?

Rudd I was very sorry to read about Mr Campbell—awful business. Must have been a terrible shock to you, Miss Norman—finding him in the bedroom like that.

Clare You haven't answered my question.

Rudd What question? Oh! I wanted to have a chat, that's all—just a friendly little chat.

Clare Mr Rudd, I've a great deal to do this morning, and I'm expecting an Inspector Cleaver to call at any moment.

Rudd Are you? That's funny, he's just left. (*Grinning*) Still, I reckon you must be busy—very busy. Silly of me, dropping in like this, out of the blue. Most inconsiderate. (*He sits in the armchair and makes himself comfortable*) I'm not usually so inconsiderate, Miss Norman, I can assure you.

Clare (*quietly, watching him*) What's all this about an insurance policy?

Rudd Your boy-friend—Larry Campbell—took out a policy with my company and I thought we might have a chat about it.

Clare (*abruptly*) When?

Rudd (*deliberately irritating her*) Do you mean when do we have the chat, or when did he take out the policy?

Clare You know perfectly well what I mean! I'm referring to the policy.

Rudd Oh—a couple of years ago, I think.

Clare You think? Don't you know?

A pause. Rudd looks at her with an impudent smile

Rudd That's a very attractive negligée, Miss Norman, if I may say so.

Clare (*angrily*) And if I may say so, what the hell's this all about? You're not from any insurance company!

Rudd (*amused*) You're dead right, I'm not.

Clare (*facing him*) Well, who are you? Who sent you here?

Rudd No-one sent me. I'm on my own. Always have been. Quite a lone wolf, in fact. Not that you'd call me a wolf, exactly. (*He reaches out and touches her negligée*) That's a very pretty colour. Reminds me of that blue dress you wore the other night.

Clare How do you know I wore a blue dress the other night?

Rudd I saw you.

Clare When?

Rudd (*smiling, obviously amused*) Oh, I saw you several times. I saw you come in and I saw you go out.

Clare (*moving towards the chair again; incredulously*) Were you watching this flat on Monday night?

Rudd (*nodding*) I was.

Clare Why?

Rudd I thought something was going to happen. I wasn't far wrong, was I?

A moment's pause

Clare (*quietly, watching him*) What did you see?

Rudd (*grinning and rising from the chair*) I saw enough to convince me that this poor chap Ryder had nothing to do with the murder.

Clare Is David Ryder a friend of yours?

Rudd (*walking towards the drinks cabinet*) I wouldn't call him a friend, exactly. I've done him one or two good turns, helped him out occasionally. (*Suddenly, turning and facing her*) He's got a very nice car, hasn't he?

Clare (*nervously, off guard*) How should I know whether he's got a very nice car?

Rudd You've seen it!

Clare (*turning away from him*) I don't know what you're talking about.

Rudd walks up behind her and stands very close

Rudd I'm talking about his Jaguar. The one with the big boot.

Clare turns and faces him again. She is angry and a shade desperate

Clare Did you follow me the other night?

Rudd I did. I did indeed, Miss Norman.

Clare (*tensely*) What else did you see?

Rudd Oh, I saw lots of things.

Clare (*angrily*) Look, I don't know what your game is, but . . .

Rudd Of course you don't! I haven't told you yet. But I'm going to . . . (*He nods towards the drinks cabinet*) Do you mind if I help myself to a drink?

Clare does not answer. She stands watching as Rudd crosses to the cabinet and mixes himself a whisky and soda

Can I get you anything?

Clare ignores the question

My word, you do look down in the dumps. (*Moving down to her*) No need to get depressed, Miss Norman. Not to worry.

Rudd drinks. There is a pause. He looks at the glass in his hand

Is this Canadian whisky?

Clare does not answer. She still stands watching him, uncertain of Rudd and of herself. He continues to drink

It's very good, whatever it is.

Rudd takes another drink and then looks up and smiles at Clare

I'm thinking of going to Canada—emigrating. Have you ever been there?

Clare (*quietly*) No, I haven't.

Rudd Sounds just the place for me. Land of opportunity—open-air life, at least so they tell me. Besides, I shouldn't be tempted to talk so much if I was in Canada. You know how it is over here. You have a few drinks, meet a few friends—Mr Ryder, perhaps. (*He looks at Clare, and drinks again*) Still, there's a snag. There always is a snag, isn't there, Clare? It is Clare, isn't it?

Clare It's Clare. What's the snag, Mr Rudd?

Rudd I need five thousand pounds.

Clare Five thou—— And where the hell do you think I'm going to get that sort of money?

Rudd (*moving down to her*) If you can't lay your hands on five thousand quid with a figure like that—God help us . . .

A long pause

Clare I'd like time to think about this.

Rudd Yes, o'course. You think about it. You can have forty-eight hours. (*He finishes his drink and puts the glass down*) I'll see you the day after tomorrow—three o'clock. (*He hesitates, then reaches out and touches her negligée*) It's my favourite colour.

Rudd grins at Clare and goes out

The front door closes. Pause. Clare moves down to the telephone. She is thoughtful and apprehensive. She stands for a little while obviously undecided what to do, then she picks up the receiver and dials

Clare (*on the telephone*) Hello? . . . Is that the "Red Lion"? . . . (*Agitatedly*) Well, what number are you? . . . Oh, I'm sorry.

She replaces the receiver and starts to dial again. She is halfway through the dialling process when the doorbell rings

She looks towards the hall, hesitates, then replaces the receiver and goes out

We hear the front door open and the sound of voices

Jo (*off*) Miss Norman—I'm Jo Mitchell. We met several months ago . . .

Clare (*off*) Yes?

Jo (*off*) I interviewed you.

Clare (*off*) Yes, I remember.

Jo (*off*) May I come in, Miss Norman? I'd like to talk to you . . .

Jo enters, followed by a somewhat puzzled Clare

Clare (*a shade unfriendly*) What is it you want to see me about?

Jo Miss Norman, I was awfully sorry to hear about—your friend, Mr Campbell. It must have been a terrible shock for you.

Clare What is it you want?

Jo Some little time ago Larry Campbell telephoned me about several letters I'd—(*obviously not very sure of herself*)—written to a friend of mine. Somehow—I don't quite know how—Mr Campbell managed to get possession of them.

Clare Well?

Jo He said he was prepared to return the letters to me but unfortunately he left for America before we had a chance to meet.

Clare I see. Well—what is it you want me to do?

Jo I was wondering if, by any chance, you've come across them?

Clare No, I'm afraid I haven't. (*After a moment; curiously*) What was in the letters, Miss Mitchell?

Jo Oh—they were just letters I wrote to a girl who—used to work for me.

Clare (*quietly*) And you say Larry offered to return them to you?

Jo Yes.

Clare looks at Jo for a moment, quietly weighing her up

Clare What did Larry want in exchange?

Jo He—didn't want anything.

Clare Then why didn't he post the letters to you?

Jo I—I don't know. I think we both felt that somehow it would be better if we—arranged to meet.

Clare I see.

Jo If you find the letters would you be kind enough to get in touch with me? (*Smiling*) That's all I'm asking.

Clare looks at her; she is cautious

Clare Yes, I will.

Jo Thank you, Miss Norman.

Jo turns towards the hall

Clare Wait a minute! There's some letters in a drawer in the bedroom. I'll go through them now if you're prepared to wait a little while.

Jo (*pleased*) Yes, of course. That's very kind of you. Thank you.

Clare goes into the bedroom

Jo takes stock of the room, then moves down to the settee. She sits on the arm of the settee and takes a packet of cigarettes from her handbag. She is lighting a cigarette when the telephone tinkles and she looks towards the bedroom. After a moment she transfers her gaze to the telephone, fully aware of the fact that Clare is talking to someone on the extension. Jo rises and moves down to the table; she stands staring at the telephone. Finally she puts her cigarette in the ashtray, and very gingerly picks up the receiver. There is a long pause. Jo listens to the telephone conversation. Suddenly she looks towards the bedroom, replaces the receiver, and quickly picking up her cigarette moves back to the sofa

Clare appears. She looks both tense and angry

Clare (*fiercely*) You were listening!

Jo Listening?

Clare Yes! Don't deny it!

Jo (*taken aback*) I assure you . . .

Clare You were listening! I heard you put the phone down!

Jo Yes, I thought perhaps the call might be for me. I left a message saying that I would be here.

Clare (*tensely*) What did you hear?

Jo Nothing. As soon as I recognized your voice I put the receiver down.

Clare (*angrily*) You're lying!

Jo What do you mean—I'm lying! I've just told you, I didn't hear anything. (*With an attempt to change the subject*) Did you find the letters?

Clare No, I didn't! (*Pointing to the telephone; even more angry than before*) What did you hear?

Jo I've told you. I didn't hear anything. And I apologize. I shouldn't have picked up the phone. I don't know why I did, it was very remiss of me. Now if you'll excuse me . . .

Jo makes a move towards the hall but Clare immediately snatches the knife from the cabinet and blocks her exit. Jo stares at the knife in amazement

Don't be a damn fool! Put that down!

Clare (*moving towards her*) Tell me what you heard . . . !

Jo (*her eyes on the knife; frightened*) I heard you say: "Is that you, Jack?" Then I—put the phone down. That's all. Nothing else . . .

Clare (*shaking her head*) I don't believe you! You heard more than that!

Jo (*backing away from Clare, towards the bedroom*) Now don't be stupid! Put that thing down!

Clare You're not leaving this room until you've told me the truth!

Jo (*with a glance towards the open bedroom door*) I've told you the truth! I simply heard you say: "Is that you, Jack?" and then I put the phone down . . .

As Clare moves closer, Jo quickly turns and makes for the bedroom, but Clare is too quick for her and for a brief moment they are locked in a brief struggle near the open door. Jo grabs at Clare in an effort to shield herself from the knife

In the ensuing struggle they both fall backwards into the bedroom. There is a terrifying scream from Jo—followed by silence

A long pause

Clare comes out of the bedroom holding the blood-stained knife. She looks distraught and desperately frightened as she backs into the room, her eyes fixed on the bedroom

Another pause

Jo slowly emerges, holding on to the bedroom door for support. Her dress is torn and smeared with blood. She is obviously in pain as she stares into the room, hardly realizing what has happened or where she is

Clare It was an accident! I didn't mean . . . Oh, God!

Jo suddenly releases her hold on the door and with a cry collapses. Clare is terrified, not sure what to do, then throwing down the knife she rushes towards the telephone—and frantically begins to dial

(*On the telephone; urgently*) . . . Is that the "Red Lion"? . . . Please put me through to Mr Jack Keller. . . . (*Pause*) Jack! Listen—there's been an accident! I've got to see you! . . . Now! Immediately! . . .

The Lights fade to a Black-out

After a little while the Lights come up on David's room. David is sitting at his desk working on a brief. A pause—then Mrs Bedford appears from the hall. She is wearing outdoor clothes and has obviously been shopping

Mrs Bedford Hope I'm not disturbing you, sir?
David No, that's all right, Mrs Bedford! Come in! (*He rises and moves around the desk*) Did you see Miss Mitchell?
Mrs Bedford No, there was no reply, so I put the note through the letter-box.
David (*concerned*) Thank you.
Mrs Bedford I think she must have gone away. I spoke to the head porter and he said he hadn't seen her.
David Thank you, Mrs Bedford. I hope it wasn't out of your way.
Mrs Bedford No, I'd arranged to meet my sister in Peter Jones and Miss Mitchell's just round the corner. (*She turns to go, then hesitates*) The porter seemed a bit concerned. He said Miss Mitchell usually lets him know when she's going away so he can tell the tradespeople.
David Did he say anything else?
Mrs Bedford No, sir. That was all.
David (*nodding*) Thank you, Mrs Bedford.

Mrs Bedford exits

David moves back to his desk; he looks thoughtful, a shade worried. He picks up the brief and looks at it absent-mindedly

Ernest Foster enters. Ernest carries a briefcase and an umbrella and appears faintly ill at ease

Hello, Ernest! Come in! I tried to get hold of you this morning but your office said you were out of town.
Ernest Yes, I got back about an hour ago. (*Indicating the document on the desk*) Is that the Liverpool brief?
David Yes, I've just been reading it. It's first class. Congratulations.

Ernest Thank you. (*He opens his case and takes out a folder*) I'm returning your notes. Sibley v. Warrington. They were a great help. In fact I don't know what we'd have done without them.

David takes the folder and puts it on his desk

What was it you wanted to see me about?

David I wondered if you'd been in touch with Jo during the past few days?

Ernest No, I haven't. My wife tried to phone her last night but there was no reply.

David I've been trying to get hold of her, but without success.

Ernest She's probably gone away for a few days. She has a brother in Scotland and she pops up there from time to time.

David Yes, I know, but she always tells her secretary when she's going.

Ernest looks at him

I've been in touch with the paper and they haven't heard a word from her. They're getting worried, she's dangerously near her deadline.

Ernest That's very odd, I must say. (*Putting down his case and umbrella*) David, when I got back to the office there was a message asking me to phone Inspector Cleaver. When I spoke to him he started questioning me about George Rudd, of all people.

David (*surprised*) Rudd?

Ernest Yes.

David Why Rudd?

Ernest You tell me! He asked me if I knew him, and when I said I did he asked me how well I knew him.

David What did you say?

Ernest I said I hardly knew him at all, but—that he did try to borrow some money from me about ten days ago.

David Did he mention the Putney case and the fact that I'd defended him?

Ernest No, but I had the feeling he knew all about it. (*Puzzled*) Why should he be interested in Rudd?

David I can't imagine why. (*A moment's pause*) Did Cleaver say anything else?

A slight pause

Ernest He wanted to know if you were a friend of Clare Norman's. She's the girl Larry Campbell's been living with. I met her at a cocktail party some little time ago and—the astute Mr Cleaver discovered this and wanted to know if you were with me. (*Pause*) David, I hate to say this, but—well, there's no point in my beating about the bush—the police think you murdered Campbell.

David Yes, I know—and it's not surprising in view of the fact that they found the murder weapon in the boot of my car. To say nothing of the fact that I'm supposed to have had an appointment with Campbell the night he was killed.

Ernest (*surprised*) Had you an appointment with him?

David No, but the police think I had. They found a note to that effect by the telephone.

Ernest Well, obviously the murderer wrote the note in order to throw suspicion on to you.

David (*shaking his head*) The note was written by Campbell.

Ernest How do you know it was written by him?

David (*somewhat irritated*) It's an accepted fact. The note's been examined by experts.

Ernest (*derisively*) Experts! David, for God's sake!

David Campbell wrote the note—there's absolutely no doubt about it!

A tiny pause

Ernest When were you supposed to have made this appointment?

David What does it matter? The point is, it was made.

Ernest How was it made?

David I imagine someone telephoned Campbell pretending to be me. Make no mistake, whoever committed this murder planned it well in advance.

A moment's pause

Ernest (*quietly*) What are you going to do, David?

David What can I do?

Ernest Well—I know what I'd do! If I were in your shoes I'd forget the Liverpool case and concentrate on my own predicament.

David (*not unfriendly*) Is that your professional advice?

Ernest To hell with my professional advice! I'm talking to you as a friend.

David To be perfectly frank, Ernest, I very nearly consulted Barrington the other day——

Ernest You couldn't do better.

David —and then, at the last moment, I changed my mind. I thought, what the hell, I'm innocent and that's that! They're bound to find the murderer sooner or later.

Ernest They're not bound to find him—or her—sooner or later, you know that as well as I do! (*He looks at his watch*) I must get back to the office. We'll talk about this later. I'll drop in for a drink sometime this evening, if that's convenient.

David Yes, do that, Ernest.

Ernest picks up his case and umbrella and moves a little towards the hall. He hesitates

Ernest I—I don't quite know how to say this . . .

David (*with a wry smile*) No, I didn't.

Ernest You—didn't what, David?

David I didn't kill Campbell, if that's what you're thinking.

Ernest (*faintly embarrassed*) Well—whoever killed him, the bastard deserved it. Still—I'm glad it wasn't you.

Ernest goes out

David returns to his desk and picks up the folder of notes. He glances at them in a perfunctory manner, his thoughts obviously elsewhere, finally putting them in a drawer

Mrs Bedford enters

Mrs Bedford Inspector Cleaver's here, Mr Ryder. He'd like a word with you.
David Yes, all right—ask him to come in.

Mrs Bedford exits

David moves behind the desk and sits in his chair. He picks up the brie and appears to be totally engrossed in it

Cleaver enters

(*Not looking up*) Sit down, Inspector. I'll be with you in a minute.

Cleaver looks at him, hesitates, then sits on the sofa. Pause. David continues to be engrossed in the document, then, after a little while, he picks up a pen and makes a note on a pad, finally putting the brief down. He knows he is going to be questioned again and he has decided to be casual, a shade cynical

David Now, what can I do for you?
Cleaver I understand you have a friend called Rudd, sir—George Rudd?
David Friend? I know a Mr Rudd, but I'd hesitate to call him a friend. Acquaintance, perhaps . . .
Cleaver But you know him?
David Yes, I know him. I've just said so.
Cleaver Correct me if I'm mistaken, but didn't you defend him on a housebreaking charge?
David You're not mistaken. I did defend him and in case you're interested, he was acquitted.
Cleaver I'm interested in anything to do with Mr Rudd. In fact, we'd very much like to interview the gentleman, but unfortunately we don't seem to be able to locate him.
David Perhaps you haven't tried hard enough.
Cleaver (*pleasantly*) There's always that possibility, sir.
David Well, I'm sorry I can't help you. I haven't the slightest idea where you can get in touch with him. As a matter of fact, I was under the impression he'd emigrated. Gone to Australia or Canada or somewhere like that.
Cleaver What gave you that impression?
David (*after a slight hesitation*) He came to see me about—oh, about a week ago. Said he was thinking of leaving the country and would I lend him some money.
Cleaver Did you lend him any?
David No, I didn't.

Cleaver Wasn't it a little odd that he should . . . pick on you, sir?

David What do you mean—"pick on me"?

Cleaver Why try to borrow money from you, Mr Ryder?

David Why not? He probably thinks I'm very well off. Most of my friends
—to say nothing of the Inland Revenue—labour under that delusion.
So why not Mr Rudd?

Cleaver Are you sure that was the purpose of his visit—just to *borrow*
money?

David I'm quite sure. He made it abundantly clear.

Cleaver He didn't try to blackmail you, by any chance?

David No, he didn't. He wasn't in a position to blackmail me. If there'd
been any suggestion of blackmail I'd have contacted you, Inspector.

Cleaver (*quietly, looking at him*) Would you, sir?

David (*unflinching*) I would indeed. (*Rising*) Now, having answered your
questions, perhaps you wouldn't mind telling me why you're interested
in Rudd? Is he in some sort of trouble?

A slight pause

Cleaver When I arrived at my office this morning Clare Norman was
waiting to see me. I imagine you've heard of Miss Norman?

David nods

She told me she'd recently had a visit from a stranger, a man called
Rudd. Rudd told her he'd been watching the flat the night Larry
Campbell was murdered and that he knew the identity of the murderer.
He offered to reveal this interesting piece of information to Miss Nor-
man for five thousand pounds.

David What did she say?

Cleaver She told him she'd think about it.

David But why should Rudd contact Clare Norman? Surely his best bet
was to blackmail the murderer?

Cleaver Yes, that's exactly what I thought, sir.

David looks at him. The telephone rings

David (*reaching for the telephone*) I've told you all I know about Rudd.
(*Dismissing him*) I'm sorry I can't be more helpful.

Cleaver rises, then hesitates, as if somewhat reluctant to be dismissed

(*On the telephone*) . . . Yes? Speaking. . . . Yes, he is—hold on. (*He
offers Cleaver the telephone*)

Cleaver (*surprised*) Oh—thank you, sir. (*Taking the telephone*) Hello?
. . . Yes, it is. . . . Oh, hello, Sergeant! What is it? (*A long pause. Darkly*)
When did this happen? . . . (*Pause*) I see. . . . (*He looks at David, who
is obviously curious*) Who identified her? . . . Yes—yes—I'm listening.
. . . (*Pause*) Is that your opinion or the doctor's? (*Another pause*) All
right—do that. I'll be with you in about half an hour.

Cleaver replaces the telephone and looks at David

(*Quietly*) When did you last see Miss Mitchell, sir?

David About three days ago, but I've been trying to get hold of her. My housekeeper even went . . . What is it, Inspector?

Cleaver (*gently, but with a serious undertone*) I'm afraid I've got some bad news for you. Miss Mitchell's dead. Her body was found on Wimbledon Common just over an hour ago.

David (*stunned*) Good God! Jo—I don't believe it!

Cleaver It's true, sir.

David But—what happened? Was it suicide?

Cleaver No, sir. It would appear that she was murdered—stabbed to death.

David But how do you know it's Jo? Who identified her?

Cleaver The man who discovered the body recognized her; he works on a local newspaper. Besides, they found her handbag. I'm afraid it's Miss Mitchell, sir. (*Pause*) What made you ask if it was suicide?

David (*miserably, dazed*) What made me ask if . . . I—I don't know. I just said the first thing that came into my head.

Cleaver (*after a moment*) Mr Ryder, we found a telegram in Larry Campbell's flat. It was from Miss Mitchell. When I questioned her about it she said she was annoyed with Campbell because he'd been trying to borrow money from her.

David Yes, I know. She told me.

Cleaver I'm afraid I didn't believe her story. I don't know whether you did, sir?

David (*after a moment's consideration*) Larry Campbell had several letters which—Jo badly wanted. They were written to a friend of hers. A girl who used to work for her. I don't know what was in the letters or how Campbell managed to get hold of them, but—I do know that Jo was—very worried about them.

Cleaver I see. (*Nodding*) I think I get the picture, Mr Ryder. Thank you.

Cleaver goes

David stands quite still, obviously deeply affected by the news of Jo's death. After a little while he mixes himself a drink. He takes the drink to the desk and sits in his chair, staring into space, occasionally drinking. When he has nearly finished the drink he makes an effort to pull himself together and, picking up the telephone, dials a number

David (*on the telephone*) This is David Ryder. . . . Mr Foster's just left me, he's on his way back to the office. Please ask him to phone me the moment he arrives. . . . Thank you. (*He replaces the receiver and buries his head in his hands*)

The Lights slowly fade to a Black-out

The Lights come up on Larry Campbell's flat. Roy Campbell is sitting on the settee reading. He is completely engrossed in the document he is holding when Clare comes out of the bedroom carrying a silk dressing-gown

Clare I've found it, Roy. It was in one of the suitcases. (*She holds up the dressing-gown*)

Roy (*rising, admiring the gown*) My word, you're right. It is a very nice one, and it looks almost new.

Clare I doubt whether he wore it more than twice. You know what Larry was like about dressing-gowns. He didn't buy them—he collected them. I was almost frightened to walk down Jermyn Street with him.

Roy takes the dressing-gown from her and examines it

Roy It's very smart, I must say.

Clare I shudder to think what he paid for it.

Roy Are you sure you can't make use of it, Clare?

Clare Absolutely certain. It's yours, Roy.

Roy Well—thank you, my dear. I can certainly do with a new one. Dilys will be delighted. She might even talk to me at breakfast.

Roy puts the dressing-gown on the settee. A moment's pause. He looks at the document again

Clare, I'm sorry, but I don't understand this Will of Larry's. I've read it half a dozen times and I'm still puzzled by it.

Clare You're not the only one, I don't understand it either.

Roy (*looking at the document*) I think Larry must have drawn it up himself.

Clare He did. I was with him when he did it. He bought the form from a stationers in Shepherds Market. I remember that day only too well. He'd just had another one of his attacks and he was feeling terribly depressed. But at least I made the poor darling laugh with that corny old joke about the millionaire and his Will. "To my son-in-law Bertie who repeatedly says 'Health before wealth'—I leave my sun lamp."

Roy smiles, then looks at the Will again

Roy Clare, would you mind if I showed my lawyer this?

Clare No, of course not. That was the point of giving it to you. You're an executor, Roy. You must do what you think is best.

Roy I'll phone him tomorrow and make an appointment. I'd like you to come along if you can manage it.

Clare There's no need for that, surely?

Roy There is, Clare. I've been talking to Dilys about you and—well, I don't want to say anything against my brother—but we both feel you've had a pretty raw deal.

Clare No, that's not true. Larry was a strange man in many ways, but— we had our moments. Let's just leave it at that.

Roy What do you think happened—the night he was killed? Do you think someone broke into the flat . . .?

Clare No-one broke into the flat. Whoever murdered Larry had a key. That's been established.

Roy How many keys are there?

Clare So far as I know, only two.

Roy Yours and Larry's?

Clare Yes.

A pause

Roy (*hesitantly*) Clare, I've never been a one for gossip, you know that. I've always felt I could safely leave that to Dilys. But just recently I've heard so many stories about Larry that I'm beginning to wonder whether I really knew him.

Clare Stories? What kind of stories?

Roy Well—for instance. It was only recently that I heard about David Ryder and what happened in the South of France.

Clare What happened in France was unfortunate. But it wasn't Larry's fault. He didn't know Evelyn Ryder was going to be taken ill. He didn't know there was going to be an accident.

Roy No, I suppose not. Still—I'm afraid the police have got their eye on Ryder, he's their number one suspect. And frankly—if you want my opinion—I think they're mistaken. I don't think he did kill Larry.

Clare He had a motive. He threatened to kill him.

Roy Yes, I know, but that was some time ago, besides . . . (*He hesitates*) I find it difficult to explain what I feel about David Ryder. In a way, it's just a hunch, I suppose, and yet . . . I know there's a doubt about his alibi, and I know they found—or are supposed to have found—the murder weapon in the boot of his car. Nevertheless, I just don't think he did it.

Clare Then who do you think did?

Roy I don't know. But let's face it, there's no shortage of suspects.

Clare (*surprised by Roy's remark*) What do you mean—no shortage of suspects? Who—apart from Ryder—would want to kill Larry?

Roy (*quietly*) Clare, Larry's dead, so let's be honest with each other. You know as well as I do that a great many people disliked my brother. Disliked him intensely.

Clare That's as maybe! But it doesn't answer my question. Apart from Ryder, who else would want to kill him?

Roy Well—Jack Keller, for one.

Clare (*after a slight hesitation; tensely*) Why Jack Keller? Why should he want to kill Larry?

Roy looks at her. He is obviously on the verge of saying something, then changes his mind. The doorbell rings. They continue looking at each other, then Clare turns towards the hall

Roy That could be Dilys. She said she might pick me up if it started to rain.

Clare exits

We hear the front door being opened

Clare (*off; surprised*) Oh, hello, Inspector!

Cleaver (*off*) Good evening, Miss Norman. Could you spare me a few minutes?

Clare (*off*) Er—yes, of course. Please come in.

Cleaver (*off*) Thank you. Not a very nice evening, I'm afraid.

Clare enters with Cleaver. The Inspector is wearing a raincoat

Roy Good evening.

Cleaver (*to Clare*) I'm sorry to disturb you. There's just one or two questions I'd like to ask you, Miss Norman.

Roy (*always uneasy in the presence of Cleaver*) I'll be off, Clare. (*He picks up the dressing-gown*)

Cleaver Please—don't run away on my account, sir. In fact, you might be able to help me. Do you happen to know a journalist called Jo Mitchell?

Roy Jo Mitchell. No, I'm afraid I don't.

Cleaver She writes a column for one of the Sunday newspapers.

Roy Yes, I know who you mean. My wife reads it regularly, every Sunday. But I've never met Miss Mitchell.

Cleaver (*pleasantly*) Then I'm afraid you can't help me, after all, sir.

A tiny pause

Roy Well—I'll be going, Clare. I'll give you a ring when I've talked to Foster.

Clare Foster?

Roy The lawyer.

Clare Oh . . .

Roy I'd like us both to see Foster. I really would.

Clare Yes, all right, Roy. If that's what you want.

Roy gives Cleaver a nod and exits

Cleaver looks at Clare; he realizes she is ill at ease

Why are you interested in Miss Mitchell, Inspector?

Cleaver She's dead. She was murdered. Her body was found on Barnes Common.

Clare Oh, my God! How awful . . .

Cleaver Did you know Miss Mitchell?

Clare (*after a moment*) Yes; very slightly. We met twice, that's all. The first time she interviewed me and the second time . . . She'd read about Larry and she wanted to know if . . . Well—apparently Larry had some letters which Miss Mitchell wanted and she asked me to try and find them for her.

Cleaver And did you find them?

Clare No, I didn't. Well, not immediately—but I've come across them since. As a matter of fact I've been trying to get hold of Miss Mitchell. I rang her office twice this morning but couldn't get any sense out of them. They didn't seem to know where she was.

Cleaver (*quietly*) Yes, they told me you'd telephoned.

Clare (*surprised*) They told you? Then you must have known about the letters! I left a message for her saying that I'd found them.

Cleaver (*unperturbed*) Yes, I know. But I wanted you to tell me about them, Miss Norman.

Clare (*just managing to suppress her annoyance*) Well—I've told you.

Cleaver (*unruffled*) May I see them? The letters . . .

Clare glares at him, then goes into the bedroom

Cleaver smiles to himself and crosses down to the table. He looks at the pad by the side of the telephone. Pause

Clare returns, carrying several letters which she hands to the Inspector

Thank you.

Cleaver opens one of the letters and reads it. He reads it very slowly, then carefully examines the envelope. Clare stands watching him; obviously uncomfortable, a shade tense. After examining the envelope Cleaver starts to read the letter again. He seems totally unaware of Clare's existence. There is a long pause

Clare (*unable to stand it any longer, breaking the silence*) You say they found Miss Mitchell—her body—on Wimbledon Common?

Cleaver looks up

Cleaver Barnes Common.
Clare Oh . . .
Cleaver No, you're quite right, Miss Norman! It was Wimbledon. (*Pleasantly*) I can't imagine why I said Barnes. (*He looks at the letter again*)

There is another pause. Clare is obviously on edge; annoyed with herself

Clare (*feeling that she ought to say something*) How was—she murdered?
Cleaver (*still concentrating on the letter*) She was stabbed to death.
Clare On the Common?
Cleaver (*looking up*) No, I don't think it happened on the Common. I think she was taken there after the murder was committed. (*Looking at the letters*) I'll take care of these.
Clare (*trying hard to play it cool*) Yes, all right.
Cleaver They're addressed to a Miss Susan Beckworth. Was she a friend of Mr Campbell's?
Clare I honestly don't know. I'd never heard of her. I don't know why Larry had the letters.
Cleaver Well—she was obviously a close friend of Miss Mitchell's, there's no doubt about that. (*Putting the letter in his pocket*) Miss Norman, thank you very much. I won't keep you any longer.

Cleaver goes out into the hall, followed by Clare

We hear the opening and closing of the front door

Clare returns. She looks distinctly worried as she moves down to the table and helps herself to a cigarette

She stands by the table, smoking the cigarette and staring into space, going over in her mind the conversation with the Inspector. Suddenly she looks at her watch and crosses to the window. She stands for a little while looking into the street, obviously expecting someone. A pause—then, as she is about to turn away from the window, she sees the person she has been expecting

Clare turns quickly and exits to the hall

There is a pause. Then we hear the front door open and Rudd's voice

Rudd (*off*) What a hell of a night!

Rudd enters, followed by Clare

Clare You're very punctual, Mr Rudd.
Rudd I'd have been a damn sight more punctual if I could have got a taxi. What happens to those buggers when it starts to rain? (*Taking off his coat*) I gather you had another visitor.
Clare Yes. (*Anxiously*) Did he see you?
Rudd I'm not that daft.
Clare Let me take your coat.

Rudd hands her the coat

Rudd It's very wet.
Clare I'll put it on a radiator in the bedroom. It'll soon dry out.

Clare takes the coat, stubs her cigarette out in the ashtray on the table, and then goes into the bedroom

Rudd looks around the room, slowly moving down to the settee

Clare returns

Would you like a drink?
Rudd Are you going to have one?
Clare Yes, I think so.
Rudd All right—I'll have a Scotch and soda.

Clare moves to the cabinet and mixes a whisky and soda and a small gin and orange. Rudd watches her. She returns to the sofa with the drinks

Rudd (*taking the drink*) Ta.
Clare Skol! (*She drinks*)
Rudd Cheers! (*He drinks, looks down at his glass for a moment, then at Clare*) What's that you're drinking?
Clare Gin and orange.
Rudd (*with a laugh*) You don't look the gin and orange type to me.
Clare Don't I?
Rudd (*with an impudent grin*) Definitely not! Dry martini—Bloody Mary—

yes! But not gin and orange. (*He drinks and then looks in the glass again*) Well, have you thought any more about my proposition?

Clare Yes, I have—and curiously enough the more I think about it, the less I like it, Mr Rudd.

Rudd (*surprised*) Oh? Why's that?

Clare You forgot to mention the alternative.

Rudd There isn't one.

Clare There's always an alternative. Supposing I don't give you this five thousand pounds? (*A little too polite*) It was five thousand, wasn't it?

Rudd (*aggressively, irritated by her manner*) It was.

Clare Well—what happens then?

Rudd Come off it! You know damn well what happens! I go to the police.

Clare And tell them what, exactly?

Rudd (*after a moment, unpleasantly*) You haven't got a very good memory, have you? Don't you remember what I told you? I watched this flat last Monday night. I saw you leave. I followed you to the garage. I saw you put the parcel in Ryder's car.

Clare (*after a moment*) What parcel?

Rudd Come on! Don't give me that!

Clare (*shaking her head*) I'm sorry, Mr Rudd. I don't believe you.

Rudd Oh—you don't?

Clare No, I don't. Why would you be watching this flat?

Rudd That's my business. (*A hidden threat*) Still, if you don't believe me, that's all right. Not to worry. Not to worry, Clare.

A pause. Clare looks at him, obviously undecided

Clare (*slowly*) If you were watching this flat on Monday night, then you must have seen . . . (*She hesitates*)

Rudd (*smiling*) Go on . . .

Clare (*bluntly*) Who did you see?

Rudd I saw more than I bargained for, I'll tell you that!

Clare (*watching him, tensely*) Who did you see?

Rudd Ryder—Roy Campbell—(*slowly, a shade amused*)—and that friend of yours.

Clare (*putting her drink down; cautiously*) What friend?

Rudd The gentleman with the scarf wrapped round his face.

Clare looks at him

Now do you believe me? (*He suddenly moves forward and takes hold of her arm*) Don't be a silly little bitch! Do you think I don't know what's going on? I know you're trying to fix Ryder—I know you want the poor bastard arrested! All right, go ahead! Why should I worry? (*He shrugs*) I couldn't care less. (*Still holding her arm*) But if I don't get that five thousand quid it won't be Ryder that'll be arrested. (*Shaking his head, emphatically*) It won't be poor bloody little Ryder . . . (*He releases her arm*)

A pause

Clare (*tensely*) I can't get you five thousand. I've tried—it's impossible.
Rudd How much can you get?

Clare hesitates for a moment

Clare Four thousand—but you'll have to wait for that! I can't get it
straight away.
Rudd (*quietly, facing her*) How long?
Clare It'll take me four or five days—a week perhaps.

A pause

Rudd (*suddenly, smiling*) I'll give you three days. Till Monday afternoon.
(*Obviously pleased with himself, he picks up his glass and, after finishing
the drink, hands it to Clare*) Now you can get me another drink—but no
soda this time.

*Clare takes the glass and crosses to the cabinet. She thoughtfully mixes
him another whisky and soda*

(*Suddenly realizing what she is doing*) I said no soda . . .
Clare Oh, I'm sorry. (*She looks at the drink and hesitates*)
Rudd (*magnanimously, pleased with himself*) That's all right.

Clare goes to him and he takes the drink

(*Watching her*) What's on your mind?
Clare (*looking up, her thoughts apparently elsewhere*) M'm? Oh, I was
just thinking. How do I know you won't go to the police when you've
got the money?
Rudd You don't. You've got to trust me. But I told you—I'm emigrating.
Going to Canada.
Clare When?
Rudd As soon as I can afford it. (*He grins and raises his glass*) Not to
worry. Not to worry, love.

*Rudd takes a long drink then looks down at the glass, obviously just a little
puzzled by the taste of the whisky. Clare stands watching him, a shade
tense. He takes another drink, then looks at the glass again, still doubtful.
Clare watches him, nervously playing with the top button of her dress as
she does so. As he looks up she casually, yet deliberately, continues playing
with the button. His thoughts slowly turn from the whisky. A moment's
pause*

I don't like that dress.
Clare (*smiling*) No?
Rudd No. Don't know why, I'm sure.
Clare Perhaps it's the colour.
Rudd (*putting down his drink*) Could be.
Clare (*still playing with the button*) It's too tight anyway . . .

*Rudd suddenly takes hold of Clare and kisses her. After a moment he runs
his right hand across her shoulder and down her back, pulling down the
zip fastener on the back of her dress*

(Playfully, struggling) Hi! What's going on?

Rudd You said it was too tight, didn't you, love?

Clare *(with a forced laugh, trying to release herself)* Yes, I know, but . . . *(She finally breaks away from him and quickly crosses to the other side of the table; she picks up his glass)* You'd better finish your drink!

Rudd gives a self-satisfied grin and takes the glass from her

Rudd I liked that thing you had on this morning—that fluffy thing. Just my cup of tea.

Clare *(a shade breathlessly, laughing)* Yes, I thought it was, Mr Rudd. *(Mimicking him)* Your favourite colour . . .

Rudd moves round the table but she laughs at him and backs towards the bedroom door, playfully holding up her hand

All right, I can take a hint!

Rudd stops; he looks at her

Finish your drink, then mix me another gin and orange . . . *(She smiles at him and turns towards the bedroom)*

Rudd *(quietly, delighted with the turn of events)* O.K. . . .

Clare goes into the bedroom

Rudd quickly finishes his drink, then, obviously very pleased with himself, he crosses to the cabinet and pours himself a whisky and mixes the gin and orange. He brings the drinks down to the table, then, after looking round the room, finally picks up several cushions and takes them over to the settee. He arranges the cushions to his satisfaction and then, as he straightens himself, he suddenly sways slightly and puts his hand over his eyes. He stands quite still, holding on to the back of the settee for support. After a little while he returns to the table. He is still dizzy and he stands by the table, his hand shielding his eyes from the light. A pause. Rudd is obviously feeling ill; he picks up the glass of whisky and is about to drink when a thought occurs to him. He looks at the glass with curiosity, holding it up to the light—then he suddenly feels another dizzy spell coming on and he replaces the glass on the table. He is worried about himself now, and a shade frightened. There is another pause

Clare appears from the bedroom. She still wears the same dress. She has a small piece of notepaper in her hand as she leans against the bedroom door

(Holding up the glass) What was in this? I feel awful—bloody awful . . .

Clare Not to worry, love.

As the drug gradually overpowers him Rudd drops the glass he is holding and sinks on to the settee. A pause—then Clare moves slowly down to the settee and picks up the glass. She stands looking at the unconscious Rudd for several seconds, then she crosses to the telephone, consults the piece of notepaper, and dials a number

A pool of light reveals David sitting at his desk working on a brief. The telephone rings and he slowly puts down his pen and answers it. His thoughts are still partly with the document he has been reading

David (*on the telephone*) David Ryder speaking . . .

Clare (*on the telephone*) Mr Ryder, this is Clare Norman. We've never met but—I expect you've heard of me. I was a friend of Larry Campbell's.

David (*alerted, his thoughts on the call*) Yes, I've heard of you, Miss Norman.

Clare I apologize for disturbing you but I'm desperately worried and I think perhaps you can help me. (*Silence. Perturbed*) Hello? . . .

David (*quietly*) I'm still here, Miss Norman.

Clare A man called Rudd came to see me, he tried to sell me some information.

David Yes, I know all about Rudd. I've seen Inspector Cleaver.

Clare (*stopping him*) No, no, forgive me, but you don't understand! I've seen Rudd again, since I spoke to the Inspector. I'm frightened of him, Mr Ryder. I just don't know what to do.

David You've been to the police, that's all you can do.

Clare (*after a tiny pause*) I don't know whether you know it or not, but —the police found a note saying you had an appointment to see Larry the night he was killed.

David Yes, I know about the note.

Clare Larry didn't write that note. Someone else wrote it and—I know who it was.

David (*instantly curious*) How do you know?

Clare Rudd told me. He was watching the flat the night Larry was murdered. Look, Mr Ryder, we can't talk about this on the phone!

David (*tensely*) Where are you? Where are you speaking from?

Clare I'm at home. Twenty-eight A Curzon Street . . .

David I'll be there in fifteen minutes!

As David quickly puts the telephone down the pool of light dies away leaving his room in total darkness

Clare replaces her receiver, and after looking at the figure of Rudd, goes into the bedroom

Pause. Rudd stirs, opens his eyes, and slowly sits upright on the settee. He groans and puts a hand to his head. He makes as if to lie down again, but fights against the desire to do so. He shakes his head and looks around the room, defying the effects of the drug. His eyes come to rest on the bedroom door. He rises unsteadily to his feet, holding on to the settee for support. He lets go of the settee and takes a step in the direction of the bedroom door. He sways, clutches erratically for the settee arm, and just saves himself from falling on to the floor. He curses under his breath as he stands there, swaying slightly, his eyes closed

The bedroom door opens and Clare enters. She is dressed in outdoor clothes and is carrying a suitcase. She stops in the doorway, staring at Rudd. She obviously expected to find him still asleep

Rudd's eyes are closed. He has not heard Clare come into the room. Clare places the suitcase on the floor, closes the bedroom door, then picks up the case and moves towards the hall. She is obviously intent on leaving the flat without Rudd knowing. Rudd suddenly utters a cry and Clare stops in her tracks. Rudd's hand grasps the settee, his foot stamping out to prevent himself from falling. Clare freezes. Rudd opens his eyes. He sees her. He stares at her in silence for a moment as if trying to recollect who she is

Rudd Where—where are you going? (*His speech is somewhat slurred*)
Clare (*putting down her case*) I'm sorry, but I've got to leave you, I've got an appointment.
Rudd (*viciously*) What the hell are you up to?

Clare stiffens as Rudd moves erratically towards her

   What have you done to me?
Clare I don't know what you mean.
Rudd Don't give me that! You put something in my drink!
Clare You're ill, Mr Rudd . . .
Rudd I'll be damned! (*Fighting to express himself*) Never ill. Never been ill in my life.
Clare You were taken ill. I've sent for a doctor.
Rudd I don't believe you—you're lying—you put something in the whisky . . .
Clare (*shaking her head*) You said you didn't feel well and then you passed out.
Rudd Don't give me that—you bitch! You tried to put one over on me!

Rudd lurches forward in an attempt to grab hold of her arm; he stumbles, sways precariously, and trips over the suitcase. Clare stares down at him, then picks up the case

Clare When you hear the doorbell, answer it. It'll be the doctor!

Clare turns and quickly goes out. The front door is heard closing as she leaves the flat

Rudd stirs, looking vaguely in the direction of the hall. After a moment he rises unsteadily to his feet. He remains there for a time, trying to clear his brain and grope his way to some course of action. Suddenly he starts to feel dizzy again, and instinctively staggers back towards the safety of the settee

The Lights fade into darkness. They come up almost immediately to reveal Rudd stretched out on the settee. The front doorbell is ringing. He stirs, looks towards the hall, then slowly rises. He is obviously feeling quite a bit better. The bell continues ringing

Rudd lurches across the room and goes out into the hall. After a moment we hear the front door open and Rudd's voice, loud and truculent

Rudd (*off*) What the hell do you want? I thought you were the doctor!

We hear voices, then the closing of the front door

> *David enters from the hall. He stands just inside the door and looks searchingly around the room. Rudd returns from the hall and leans wearily against the wall. He surveys David with puzzled eyes*

David You say Miss Norman's out?

Rudd Yes, she's just left . . .

David (*puzzled*) Well—where has she gone?

Rudd I don't know where she's gone! I've been feeling rotten. She told me she'd sent for a doctor! (*Moving down to the settee*) The little bitch was lying . . .

David (*annoyed*) But she phoned me, only fifteen minutes ago. I was supposed to meet her here!

Rudd I don't know anything about that. (*Holding his head*) I don't know anything about anything—except that my blasted head's aching all the time!

David How long have you been here?

Rudd God knows!

David Were you here when she phoned me?

Rudd How the devil do I know? I've been spark out . . .

David looks at Rudd and jumps to the conclusion he has been drinking

David Miss Norman said you spoke to her about the appointment I was supposed to have made.

Rudd What appointment?

David With Larry Campbell . . .

Rudd I didn't talk to her about anything. How the hell could I? (*Pointing to the whisky decanter*) I wasn't here five minutes before she slipped me a dose of that stuff. The little bitch . . .

David moves to the drinks cabinet; he picks up the decanter

It's loaded—like a bloody cannon.

David looks at the decanter then slowly replaces it

David (*quietly, yet with authority*) The last time we met you told me you were watching this flat the night Campbell was murdered.

Rudd Well?

David If you were, then you saw the murderer. You must have done.

Rudd (*nervously, a shade frightened by David's manner*) No—no, I didn't. I didn't see anything.

David Rudd, I think there's something you ought to know. Miss Norman's been to the police.

Rudd (*staggered*) What!

David She told the Inspector about your visit.

Rudd moves down to David, staring at him in astonishment

Rudd Why the stupid little bitch! Why in God's name did she do a bloody silly thing like that! (*With a sudden thought*) That woman's up to something! That's why she's got you here! I'm getting my coat and getting to hell out of here!

Rudd pushes David aside and goes into the bedroom

David hesitates, then he too makes a decision and moves towards the telephone. He has just picked up the receiver when a loud protesting cry comes from the bedroom quickly followed by a shot. An astonished David slams down the telephone and rushes towards the open bedroom door. He stops dead, staring into the other room

Larry Campbell comes out of the bedroom. He carries an overcoat and scarf and holds a gun in his right hand

There is a pause as the two men stand staring at each other

Larry I'll bet you look even more astonished than I did, the night you tried to kill me.

David (*quietly, slowly recovering from the shock of seeing Larry*) What happened that night?

Larry You scared the living daylight out of me—but you made me think. You made me realize that "death" was the only answer to my problems. And believe me, I had problems, Ryder. (*Moving to the settee*) After you left I had another visitor. Jack Keller. A miserable sonofabitch who just wanted to borrow money. I reckon I did the poor bastard a favour; making sure his body would be mistaken for mine. (*Putting down his coat and scarf*) Fortunately, Keller lived alone, over a pub in Shere Street. I sent the landlord a telegram. The "long awaited" job had turned up at last. Later I assumed Keller's identity and went into hiding. In fact, everything was going along nicely, very nicely—(*angrily*)—until Rudd and the inquisitive Miss Mitchell loused things up!

David Why "inquisitive" Miss Mitchell?

Larry She picked up the phone whilst Clare was talking to me. Whether she recognized my voice or not, I don't know. Clare seemed to think she did, so . . .

David So what?

Larry Clare lost her temper, and panicked. (*He shrugs*) It was unfortunate.

Pause

David And now, what happens?

Larry I thought barristers were quick thinkers, a jump ahead of everyone else.

David I'm supposed to have been blackmailed by Rudd, so I killed him. Is that the situation?

Larry makes no comment

After which, no doubt, I committed suicide?

Larry That's the situation.

David looks at·him for a moment, then, to Larry's amazement, starts to laugh

David You must be joking! You don't really think you'll get away with this?

Larry Why shouldn't I get away with it? So far as the police are concerned I'm dead. In less than two hours I'll be with Clare and out of the country. By this time tomorrow, believe it or not, I'll have picked up the best part of three hundred thousand dollars.

David Will you? I doubt it. I doubt it very much.

Larry looks at him, surprised by the reaction to his statement

You see, it isn't quite as simple as that.

Larry What do you mean?

David I mean—unfortunately for you, your girl-friend overlooked something.

Larry (*after a moment*) Overlooked something?

David Yes. Don't you know what I mean?

Larry No, I don't know what you mean!

David (*pleasantly*) Come now, surely you must have some idea of what I'm referring to.

Larry I haven't the slightest idea what you're referring to! What did Clare overlook?

As David continues to smile at him

Tell me!

A tiny pause

David (*very convincingly, almost believing his own words*) Very well. I'll tell you. But I'm afraid you're not going to like it. Approximately twenty-four hours ago I received a telephone call from . . . (*With a startled look over Larry's shoulder, towards the bedroom*) Rudd!!

Completely taken-in by David's ruse, Larry half-turns towards the bedroom. David immediately springs forward, viciously chopping the gun out of Larry's hand. The two men come to grips—both desperately trying to stop each other from reaching the gun. David's hand is now on the revolver and Larry lashes out in a wild attempt to stop him from gaining possession of it, but in doing so he slips and David quickly points the gun at him. There is a long pause

Larry (*quietly*) Put that gun down. You know as well as I do that you're not going to use it.

David What makes you think I'm not going to use it?

Larry You didn't use it before and you're not going to use it now.

David You think I'm frightened of the consequences, is that it?

Larry I think you're frightened of yourself, Ryder. People like you just don't take the law into their own hands. Now do as I say and put that thing down, or there'll be an accident.

Another pause. Larry continues staring at the gun, then with a shrug he crosses to the settee and leisurely picks up his coat and scarf. He is very sure of himself again; there is even a suggestion of forced impudence about him

David Campbell, there's something I want to tell you, and this time I'm not bluffing. So please sit down.

Larry turns, surprised by David's politeness. He sits on the arm of the settee

Larry Well—what is it you want to tell me?

David A few minutes ago you were very frank with me. You admitted that you intended to shoot me and make it look like suicide. Well—now I think it only fair that I should be equally frank with you. (*Slowly, and with an unmistakable note of ruthlessness*) If you rise from that settee, if you move so much as one foot away from where you're sitting now, I shall kill you.

Larry stares at David in amazement. Pause

Larry And what happens if you do kill me? If I couldn't get away with it, what makes you think you will?

David After I've shot you I shall telephone Cleaver. I shall tell him that you're here, in this flat, alive. I shall tell him we've just had a struggle, that you tried to shoot me, and that I managed to get possession of the gun.

Larry And then . . . ?

David It'll be ten minutes at least before the police get here, by which time—by which time there will have been an unfortunate accident, Mr Campbell.

Larry And you think Cleaver will believe that story?

David I think so. It's surprising how convincing I can be when the occasion demands it. Apart from which, of course, the room will be in a shambles and I shall certainly look like a man who's been fighting for his life.

Pause

Larry You won't do it, Ryder. People like you never do.

David That's where you're wrong! There comes a time for people like me . . .

As David finishes speaking the telephone rings. Larry gives a sudden start, then looks across at the telephone. There is a long pause. Larry's eyes are now back on David and the gun; trying to weigh up the true situation. He is desperately undecided whether to risk it, and move towards the telephone. Pause. The telephone continues ringing. Larry is still not a hundred per cent sure that David is deadly serious. Pause. Larry looks at the telephone, then at David. The telephone continues ringing. There is a tense pause. Larry suddenly makes a slight gesture, just a flicker of movement

(*Inexorably*) Move one foot away from that settee and I shall kill you.

Larry freezes. He realizes now that David has every intention of carrying out his threat. There is another pause. David backs towards the table, reaches out and picks up the telephone. His eyes and the gun are still fixed on Larry

(*On the telephone*) Yes? . . . Oh, hello, Inspector! This is David Ryder. . . . No, I'm afraid you can't, Miss Norman's just left for the airport. . . . What am I doing here? That's a good question! Why don't you come down here and find out? . . . And don't be too long, Cleaver, or I really will commit a murder this time. (*With the suggestion of a smile*) The same one . . .

CURTAIN

FURNITURE AND PROPERTY LIST

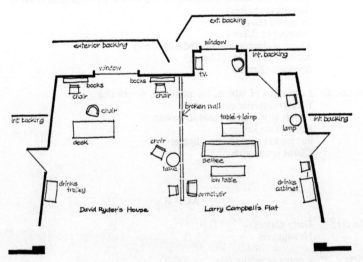

ACT I

On stage: **RYDER'S ROOM**

Desk. *On it:* 2 telephones, lamp, papers, briefs, lamp, writing materials, photographs, ashtray. *In drawers:* cigar-box containing revolver, folder of papers

Drinks trolley. *On it:* various drinks, including whisky, glasses

2 sections of bookshelves in walls, with assorted books including legal volumes

Wing chair. *In it:* newspaper

3 small chairs

Desk chair

Occasional table. *On it:* ashtray

Long window curtains

Carpet

CAMPBELL'S ROOM (Swedish-style furnishings)

Settee. *On it:* cushions

Low coffee table. *On it:* box of cigarettes, lighter, ashtray, telephone, pad, pencil, magazines, document in large envelope under magazines

Settee table. *On it:* lamp

Standard lamp

Drinks cabinet. *On it:* whisky, brandy, gin, orange juice, soda syphon, various glasses, lamp. *In drawer:* knife

3 small chairs

2 armchairs. *On them:* cushions

Television set. *Below it:* wastepaper-basket
Carpet
Window curtains

Off stage: Suitcase containing statuette, valise, bundle of magazines **(Larry)**
Attaché case **(Roy)**
Telegram **(Boy)**
Newspaper **(Clare)**
Vacuum cleaner, dusters **(Mrs Bedford)**
Attaché case, note **(Cleaver)**
Briefcase **(Ernest)**

Personal: **Larry:** box of tablets, fountain pen, wristwatch
Ernest: cigarette case, lighter
David: wristwatch, ticket in envelope
Rudd: Yale key
Jo: packet of cigarettes, lighter
Clare: wristwatch

ACT II

Strike: Dirty glasses
Newspapers

Set: Rooms generally tidy
Pile of letters and receipts on floor
Drawer on floor
Roy's hat and coat on settee back

Off stage: Brown paper parcel **(Roy)**
Cardboard box containing negligée and mules **(Clare)**
Blood saucer for knife **(Clare)**
Briefcase, umbrella **(Ernest)**
Folder of notes in briefcase **(Ernest)**
Document **(Roy)**
Silk dressing-gown **(Clare)**
Opened letters **(Clare)**
Piece of notepaper **(Clare)**
Suitcase **(Clare)**
Gun **(Larry)**

LIGHTING PLOT

Property fittings required: CAMPBELL'S FLAT: 3 Swedish-style lamps, wall
   brackets, television effect; RYDER'S HOUSE: table lamp, wall brackets
Interior. 2 living-rooms (split set). The same scene throughout

ACT I
To open: Black-out

Cue 1	After CURTAIN up	(Page 1)
	Bring up to morning light in **Campbell's** *room*	
Cue 2	**Larry** settles on cushion	(Page 2)
	Fade on **Campbell's** *room; bring up to evening lighting in* **Ryder's** *room—all practicals on*	
Cue 3	**David** looks at photograph	(Page 9)
	Fade on **Ryder's** *room; bring up to evening light in* **Campbell's** *room—wall brackets on*	
Cue 4	**Larry** turns out main light and turns on lamp	(Page 17)
	Bring lighting down to covering Spot	
Cue 5	**Larry** turns on television	(Page 17)
	Pause, then fade in television effect	
Cue 6	As **David** stares down at **Larry**	(Page 18)
	Fade lighting and television in **Campbell's** *room; bring up lighting in* **Ryder's** *room to daylight*	
Cue 7	**Cleaver** replaces statuette in attaché case	(Page 33)
	Fade to Black-out	

ACT II
To open: Black-out

Cue 8	After CURTAIN up	(Page 35)
	Bring up lighting in **Campbell's** *room to morning light*	
Cue 9	**Clare:** "Now! Immediately!"	(Page 44)
	Fade lighting on **Campbell's** *room; after a pause, bring up to morning light in* **Ryder's** *room*	
Cue 10	**David** buries head in hands	(Page 49)
	Fade lighting in **Ryder's** *room; bring up to afternoon light in* **Campbell's** *room*	
Cue 11	**Clare** dials number	(Page 57)
	Bring up Spot on **Ryder's** *desk*	
Cue 12	**David** puts down receiver	(Page 58)
	Fade spot	
Cue 13	**Rudd** staggers to sofa	(Page 59)
	Fade to Black-out	
Cue 14	Immediately following	(Page 59)
	Bring up to previous lighting	

EFFECTS PLOT

ACT I

ACT II

MADE AND PRINTED IN GREAT BRITAIN BY
LATIMER TREND & COMPANY LTD PLYMOUTH

MADE IN ENGLAND